Suzi QUATRO

THROUGH MY PAIN

Poetry and Reminiscences

Volume Three

new haven
publishing

Published 2025

NEW HAVEN PUBLISHING LTD

www.newhavenpublishingltd.com

newhavenpublishing@gmail.com

Cover design © Pete Cunliffe

pcunliffe@blueyonder.co.uk

newhaven
publishing

ISBN: 978-1-915975-19-5

Contents

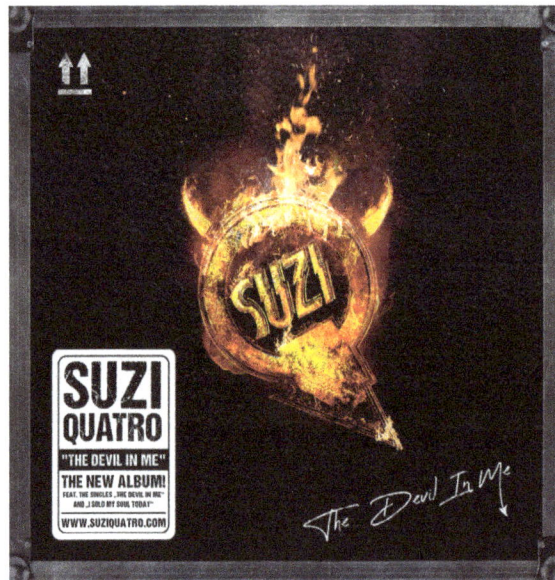

Cover photos (artwork Peter Cunliffe) are taken from snaps from the video of 'I sold my soul today', a track on my 2021 album pictured above, 'The Devil In Me'.

Suzi QUATRO

THROUGH MY PAIN

Prologue

Photo Credit: James Nuttal

s it possible that I am on my third published poetry book? This world never stops inspiring me. The time span for this collection is about 3 years give or take.

Feeling, laughing, crying, examining, criticising, regretting, and everything in between. I am in my 74th year as I write these opening remarks. I am in my sixtieth year in 'show business', which I have dedicated my entire life to. And that includes everything that being an entertainer, communicator, and creator allows me to be. I am unashamedly an 'artiste', always reaching for the next pinnacle and hoping I never actually get there.

What would I do then? After *THROUGH MY EYES*, and *THROUGH MY HEART*, there was no other appropriate title but **THROUGH MY PAIN**, which begins and ends this offering completing 'this' trilogy, poetically speaking.

A word-driven mind can be heaven or hell, depending on your disposition.

Made even more precarious when your word-driven mind is connected directly to your emotion-driven heart.

Which means there is no safe place to hide.

Acting hard as nails, answering back with a bite that is 'worse than your bark', then running out of steam, turning your back on the argument and sinking down into a swivel chair as the tears flow.

Once they subside, out comes the poem.

THROUGH MY PAIN
(Part 1)

PAIN IS YOUR BEGINNING, PAIN IS AT YOUR END,
PAIN IS YOUR ENEMY, DISGUISED AS YOUR FRIEND.
IN INNOCENT SLUMBER YOU DREAMT,
SWEET CHILD, BELIEVING IN MIRACLES.
NOW FACED WITH THE LIFE YOU'VE LED.

SELFISH FOOLISH AND NAIEVE,
PART OF YOUR CHARM IT'S BEEN SAID.
HOW COULD YOU CONCEIVE THIS POLARITY,
COULD SLUMBER SO PEACEFUL IN YOUR BED,
AND CO-EXIST IN SOLIDARITY.

STTEALING YOUR PEACE OF MIND,
LAYING SOFT BETWEEN THE SHEETS.
CRASHING LOUD LIKE THUNDER,
OH, HOW YOUR POOR HEART BEATS,
IN AWE, IN DESPAIR, AS YOU WONDER.

IF PAIN IS THE BEGINNING AND PAIN WILL BE MY END
I WILL WELCOME MY ENEMY; I WILL GREET MY OLD FRIEND.
TAKE ME TO THE RIVER, LET IT STORM, GOD, LET IT RAIN.
WASH AWAY MY SINS AND CLEANSE MY GUILT,
SO, I CAN DREAM AND HOPE AGAIN.

Australia, back stage RHST2024,
Rick Nielsen (Cheap Trick), me, Rainer.

IF YOU'VE LOVED ONCE, YOU CAN LOVE AGAIN

IF YOU'VE LOVED ONCE, YOU CAN LOVE AGAIN,
SO, TAKE MY HAND AND LET OUR FLIGHT BEGIN
TEARS OVER HAPPY SNAPSHOTS,
DOWN THE VALLEY THEN OVER THE HILL TOPS.
IF YOU'VE LOVED ONCE, YOU CAN LOVE AGAIN.

MY WHOLE LIFE ANTICIPATING,
MY WHOLE LIFE, DREAMING AND WAITING.
IN THE DARKNESS LOVE'S LIGHT SHINES THROUGH,
AND I SEE THE MAN THAT IS YOU.
AND THAT MAN IS INTOXICATING.

IF YOU'VE LOVED ONCE YOU CAN LOVE AGAIN,
SO LET THE GAMES BEGIN.
IN THE BATTLE TO HAVE THE LAST WORD,
NEITHER ONE OF US CAN BE HEARD.
YES, IF YOU'VE LOVED ONCE, YOU CAN,
YOU SHOULD, YOU COULD, YOU WILL,
LOVE AGAIN.

There are many songs, poems, books, movies, with this theme.

We have all been there in relationships which is where we are truly tested. How much do we take? How much can we keep believing? When is it time to throw in the towel?

Well folks... I am a stayer. That's how I am wired, until of course, there is no choice and I do indeed walk away, and I don't look back.

My favourite lines in this stanza are the final two. Says it all.

LOVE IS A FOUR LETTER WORD

YOUR LOVED ONE WANTS TO WALK AWAY,
BUT YOUR HEART STILL BEATS STEADY AND STRONG.
DO YOU BEG AND PLEAD, PLEASE STAY, PLEASE STAY.
OR SIMPLY FILE IT UNDER WRONG?

HOW CAN PRIDE MAKE A STAND,
WHEN HUMILIATION HAS TAKEN THE LEAD?
YOUR LOST IN LUSTS NEVER-NEVER LAND.
THERE IS NO ADVICE YOU CAN HEED.

AND YET THERE IS SOMETHING TO BE SAID
FOR THOSE WHO ARE 'ABLE' TO BELIEVE.
THAT EVERYTHING HAPPENS FOR A REASON,
EVEN WHEN THAT REASON, GETS UP AND LEAVES!

ONCE THE ACTORS HAVE PLAYED THEIR PARTS,
AND THE SCRIPT HAS BEEN TOSSED ASIDE,
WILL THE TEARS YOU CRY RELEASE YOU?
OR WILL YOU RUN AWAY AND HIDE?

LOVE IS A FOUR-LETTER WORD, OVERUSED,
BY PEOPLE WITH NO IDEA WHAT IT MEANS.
LOVE IS A FOUR-LETTER WORD, MUCH ABUSED,
DON'T LET THAT MIS-USE DICTATE 'YOUR' CLOSING SCENE.

FOR EVEN WHEN IT ALL GOES WRONG,
AND YOU'RE STANDING THERE, WIND BLOWN AND BATTERED,
YOU WILL ONE DAY SING A DIFFERENT SONG,
AND KNOW YOU 'LOVED' WHEN IT MATTERED.

Acceptance

Accept the fact
and results of getting older.

Accept the different
journeys we all take in life.

Accept the different
perspectives these journeys produce.

Accept the rights of others
to agree to disagree.

Accept that you don't have to
take everything personally.

Accept that not everyone is going to
love you, the way you choose..

That even when fractured, love can remain.
That some people have changed, and will never be the same.
That *you* have changed, and will never be the same.
That acceptance is everything,
and you must find *your* peace within.

S.Quatro 31.12.23

(written recently and a perfect intro into the next poem)

Just past midnight. As the house and the inhabitants sleep, I come alive.

Been my habit since a young girl. To bed at the appointed hour according to my age. Hearing the t.v. blaring, conversations, arguments, people walking back and forth. The soundtrack of my life. Secure enough to sleep.

Then the magic wand of silence awakens me. I arise and wander the house, claiming every room for my own. It was heaven then and its heaven now.

My thoughts fly free, I feel free, I am free. Free of what, you ask.

Free of the feeling that I am not free, as my free spirit floats through the house.

TONIGHT, I PONDER

IN THE FAMILY ROOM WATCHING T.V.
LONG AFTER THE MIDNIGHT HOUR,
THINKING ABOUT MY LIFE, RIGHT TURNS AND WRONG. THE LOSS
OF POWER.
COULD I HAVE AVOIDED TRAGEDY?
MADE A SMALLER INCISION?
COULD I HAVE HELD ON TO THE GOOD STUFF,
MADE A DIFFERENT DECISION?
DECISIONS THAT ALWAYS SEEM RIGHT, IN THE MOMENT, HA!!!
DON'T THEY JUST.
PROBLEM IS THAT MOMENT APPEARS BRIEFLY
AND DISAPPEARS TOO QUICK TO KNOW.
THEN THE CHOICE IS GONE, AND YOU'RE BUST.
FAMILY, SUCH A HUGE WORD THAT MEANS EVERYTHING.
YOU CANNOT ESCAPE IT, YOU CANNOT OUTWIT IT,
YOU CAN NEVER DENY IT.
MOM, DAD, SISTERS, BROTHERS, CHILDREN, GRANCHILDREN,
THEY ARE 'EVERYTHING, EVERYTHING, EVERYTHING.'
FROM AS LONG AS YOU CAN REMEMBER
IT'S THE WAY IT IS.
THEN YOU ALL SEPARATE AND YOU WALK YOUR OWN PATH,
NO MATTER THE OUTCOME. YOU PONDER, YOU WONDER,
YOU WANDER, AND THEN SOME.
I SIT AFTER THE MIDNIGHT HOUR, ANALYSING,
THINKING AND CRYING.

KNOWING IN THE DEEPEST PART OF ME,

I REGRET MY FAMILY DYING.

AND I DON'T MEAN DYING IN THE GRAVE,

I MEAN DYING WHILE THEY ARE ALIVE!

I SWEAR TO GOD I WILL UNITE ALL THE PLAYERS,

IF IT'S THE LAST DAMN THING I DO.

OR DIE TRYING TO MAKE MY HOPES COME TRUE.

TONIGHT, I PONDER WITH A GLASSFUL OF WINE

TONIGHT, I PONDER, TILL MY PONDERING IS THROUGH.

*The last part of this poem, from "
I swear to God I will unite all the players..."
became a poem in its own right.*

Having 750 pairs of shades makes it difficult to choose.
Are they grey or blue? (inside joke)

I was awarded 'rear of the year' in 1981, and have a golden plaque to prove it.

It was my part in 'Minder' that won me this accolade.

The scene of me walking by the river with Dennis in my tight fitting blue jeans. As Mickie Most once said to me, "you wear jeans like nobody else". Makes me wonder, do people prefer my A side or my B side.

The question is rhetorical. Here comes the poem.

Ps. I always try to back into a room if I can!

Pps. There has 'not' been silence yet, when I turn my back on the audience and and shake my ass.

Ppss. Long may it continue.

Pppss "ass" me no questions and I'll tell you no lies

Finished now. .

JEAN/JEANIE

YOUR FAVOURITE JEANS, FOR THE SCRAP HEAP?
SOMEHOW YOU JUST CAN'T DO IT.
MANY MEMORIES STUFFED IN THOSE POCKETS
WITH RUSTED ZIPPERS,
THREADS RUNNING THROUGH IT.

THE REFLECTION OF A PERFECT FIT,
LIKE A GLOVE HUGGING YOU TIGHT.
FOR SOME REASON YOU NEED TO BUY THEM,
SWEET ILLUSION,
SWEET PERFECTION.

YOU LOOK GOOD ENOUGH TO EAT,
NO MATTER HOW DIM THIS REFLECTION.
YOU BASK IN THE WARMTH OF YOUR HEAT,
THEN YOU PULL ON YOUR OLD PAIR.

WALKING BOLDLY TO THE CASHIER,
IN COMFORTABLE JEANS WITH FRAYED EDGES,
STILL, IT'S NICE TO HAVE A SPARE.

Me being Me... well, who the hell else can I be?

Sometimes the rhyme is short and sweet,
sometimes it rambles on and on.

I am not in control of which way the words
flow, I am simply taking down dictation from
the muses in heaven and I humbly thank them
for allowing me to do so.

I don't understand where it comes from, but
I have no intention of questioning my sources.

I actually don't know where this next one
came from.

No title, written on a tiny scrappy bit of
paper.

But, mine is not to question.

LIFELESS FACES, NAKED IN THE WIND
GENTLE BREEZES BLOW MY THOUGHTS, I BEGIN.
SMOKE AND SHADOWS, CLOUDING UP MY MIND
LONELY FOOTSTEPS, WALK ONE STEP BEHIND

ENDLESS SPACES FADING BLACK TO GREY
BURIED TREASURES, LOST TO YESTERDAY.
YEARNING FOR THAT LIFE I USED TO LEAD,
FROZEN MEMORIES, 'I' WATCH 'ME' BLEED.

File this one under 'heavy man, heavy'!

A mural created for an event in Chelmsford, and I was able to get hold of it. It is in my garage ready for the next video shoot..

Damn good eh!

(This was also written recently, midnight ramblings when my thoughts run wild)

Difficult times, up late, quiet, all alone but not alone.

Staring out of the white lace curtains, street lamp lighting the room just enough so I need nothing more. If something is lighting the way be it spiritual, illusion or that devil called reality, you need no other light.

We all age. You can do it joyfully, or miserably. I choose joy. But we are all unique and see the world as we see it, with our own morals, expectations, quirks, needs, hopes and desires.

And these differences do and will cause harsh words to be thrown back and forth, my God, even soulmates argue! And if they don't, then they aren't soul mates.

Non- negotiable. Don't argue with me, just read on.

MY LIFE

1957 OR THERE ABOUTS, STICKS LIKE GLUE
ASLEEP IN MY HOUSE, MY HEART,
4 BEDROOMS, 5 CHILDREN, THEM AND YOU.
SHARING WITH SISTERS OR BROTHER,
MOM AND DAD, OF COURSE SLEPT ALONE.
SOME SIBLINGS GOT LUCKY,
CLAIMING SPACE OF THEIR OWN.
NEVER A RADIO OR RECORD PLAYER, OH NO,
MY OWN BIRTHDAY PARTY ALSO WENT ASTRAY.
NEVER KNOWING WHERE TO GO,
OR WITH WHICH CHILDREN I SHOULD PLAY.
ELDER SISTER MARRIED, ROOM HAD TO BE MADE.
3 OF US NOW IN THE BIGGEST BEDROOM,
IT WAS A HUMAN PARADE.
ELDERS SISTER/HUBBY, MOVED OUT,
BROTHER MARRIED, MOVED IN.
ANOTHER GRANDCHILD, A CROWDED BEDROOM,
I BAGGED THE OPPOSITE ROOM, PEACE WITHIN.
DECORATED HOW I WISHED
PULL OUT COUCH, SMALL T.V.
MY PRIVATE SPACE TO CAMP IN, FINALLY, A REALITY
I LOVED THIS ROOM BECAUSE IT WAS 'MINE',
NOT SURE WHERE THE OTHERS SLEPT.
BUT, THAT SENSE OF FREEDOM, I'VE KEPT.
ELDER SISTER, SHE WENT OFF TO COLLEGE
THEN, IN OUR NEW PINK HOME MY DAD HAD BUILT.
A MIRACLE, MY OWN ROOM, AGAIN.. NO GUILT.
ALLOWED TO CHOOSE THE WALL PAPER
GREEN FLOWERS AND TREES TO TOUCH
FREEDOM, PEACE, IT WAS OVER WHELMING,
ALMOST BUT NOT QUITE, TOO MUCH.
A PLACE NO ONE COULD INVADE. MINE AND MINE ALONE

MY BELONGINGS IN THE CLOSET. DRAWERS OF MY OWN.
UNEXPECTEDLY SISTER RETURNED,
PULL OUT COUCH IN DAD'S OFFICE.
SOON SLEEPING IN 'MY' ROOM WITH ME, TEMPORARY?
AN EMPTY PROMISE. DOWNSTAIRS TO THE BASEMENT,
NEW BED, NEW DRAWERS, NEW NIGHTSTAND.
MY CELLAR OF REFUGE, MY SANCTUARY.
LIFE CONTINUED IN OUR 'ALL GIRL' BAND,
FAVOURITE ARTISTS ON THE WALL, DYLAN,
OTIS AND DONOVAN.
INCENSE BURNING, DISSECTING LYRICS, INHALING,
INTOXICATING, ATMOSPHERIC.
MANY HOURS DREAMING MY DREAM,
CONTINUING LIFE IN 'SHOW BIZ'
KNOWING INSIDE I WOULD SUCCEED,
THAT TAP ON THE SHOULDER,
MY BUCKS FIZZ. A CONUNDRUM,
NOT ONE NIGHT IN THAT BED,
WENT FOR THE DREAM INSTEAD.
NEVER SLEEP IN THE BASEMENT,
WHEN A HIGHER HUNGER CAN BE FED.

Leather bikini, Australia, had to be done.

Relationships go through various stages, the attraction, the flirtation, the coming together taking a chance on love, the getting to know each other, marking boundaries, learning which buttons not to push, or, which button to push depending on the situation, the argument phase which sometimes goes on for years when one or the other's health is not so good.

During these times you have to seriously consider your own future. YOUR boundaries, YOUR needs, YOUR hopes, YOUR desires and still have compassion. Because of your closeness you do become the punching bag, not literally! And, you just have to take it until its over.

This poem was written during an argument phase, until it phased out! The love remained.

LIGHT AND SHADE

FROM THE WARMTH OF LOVE TO THE COLD AND DARK
FROM A SMILING HEART TO THE BLEAK AND STARK.
A MATCH MADE IN HEAVEN BRIGHT LIGHTS BRIGADE
A LESSON IN MADNESS THIS LIGHT AND SHADE.

IT'S A QUESTION OF COURAGE WITHIN DISCOURAGE
IT'S A QUESTION OF BELIEF WITHIN DIS-BELIEF.
FAITH IS ALWAYS THE BAROMETER WE USE,
WHICH REVEALS THE TRUTH WITHIN THE ABUSE.

WHEN A PERSON BECOMES FRAIL, ANGRY AND TIRED,
AND LASHES OUT AT THE STRONG, TILL HIS FIGHT HAS
EXPIRED, AND THE RECIPIENT TAKES IT ON THE CHIN
KNOWING RETALIATION IS FOR SURE, A NO WIN

A MATCH MADE IN HEAVEN LOVERS ENTWINED
ONE BLACK, ONE WHITE, THEIR DESTINY SIGNED.
THE BILL IS PRESENTED A DEBT UNPAID,
A LESSON IN MADNESS THIS LIGHT AND SHADE

Rainer, me, Alice and Sheryl, gigging together again in Germany 2024, last tour together was 1975, a long time between drinks! (I watched them fall in love)

I made a little experiment.

I posted some stanzas on my facebook pages asking for everyone to comment. Opinions, reactions, whatever, all were welcome.

It was so interesting to see how these few lines triggered people in very different ways.

If you missed it, you can do it now instead.
Let's see which way 'you' turn.

Being a typical Gemini, ruling planet Mercury, the planet of communication, which means...

Words are the tools I use. Ready, 1, 2, 3.. Go!!!

STANZA NUMBER 1

WHEN TROUBLE KNOCKS ON YOUR DOOR,
DO YOU LET IT IN?
OR DO YOU SWITCH OFF ALL THE LIGHTS,
AND PRETEND YOU'RE NOT IN?

STANZA NUMBER 2

WE ARE ALL BORN WITH A SELL-BY DATE
AS WE HEAD TOWARDS OUR FINAL BREATH.
WOULD YOU LIKE TO KNOW THE EXACT MOMENT?
OR PREFER TO BE SURPRISED BY DEATH.

The Faroe Islands, just the landscape seems appropriate.

X-RAY VISION

IF YOU COULD SEE 'NEATH THE LAYERS
OF YOUR MANY DISAPPOINTMENTS
COULD THE AUDIENCE AND THE PLAYERS
READ THE SCRIPT FOR MY ENJOYMENT?
COULD I DISSECT THE CONSTANT CONFLICT,
THIS NEED TO PUSH EVERYONE'S BUTTONS?
LIKE A NUCLEAR DECLARATION,
WE ARE ALL BUT LAMBS DRESSED AS MUTTON.
IT'S SAD, TO ACHIEVE SO MUCH,
SUCH WEALTH, YOU'VE WON THE GAME.
YET NONE OF IT MAKES YOU HAPPY,
NOT THE CARS, THE WINE, OR FICKLE 'FAME'.
AND I WONDER WHAT IS IT WE'RE ALL LOOKING FOR?
THIS LONELY EXISTANCE WE CALL HOME.
AN UNCOMFORTABLE COUCH, AN UNUSED KITCHEN,
EMPTY WORLD, EMPTY LIFE, EMPTY POEM
MONEY CAN'T BUY YOU LOVE,
CLICHED THOUGH IT MAY BE.
IT CAN BUY YOU MORE COMFORTABLE SADNESS,
BUT THAT'S ALL IT CAN EVER BE.
IF I HAD X RAY VISION
IF I COULD SOMEHOW MAKE IT PLAIN.
I'D MAKE THE DECISION,
AND CUT AWAY ALL THE PAIN.
BUT I AM ONLY HUMAN
WITH WANTS AND NEEDS OF MY OWN.
I CAN'T COMPLETE YOUR PICTURE,
YOUR HEART BEATS ALONE.
YET I SEE YOU AS YOU ARE,
THERE IS SO MUCH GOOD INSIDE.
BURIED BY YOUR ANGER,
SMOTHERED IN YOUR PRIDE.
IF I HAD X RAY VISION
A MAGIC WAND TO WAVE,
I WOULD DESTROY YOUR DEMONS,
WE'D FACE THEM, TOGETHER, BRAVE.
BUT ALL I CAN DO IS LOVE YOU,
RIDE THE WAVES OF YOUR DISCONTENT.
IF I COULD PURCHASE X-RAY VISION
IT WOULD BE MONEY VERY WELL SPENT.

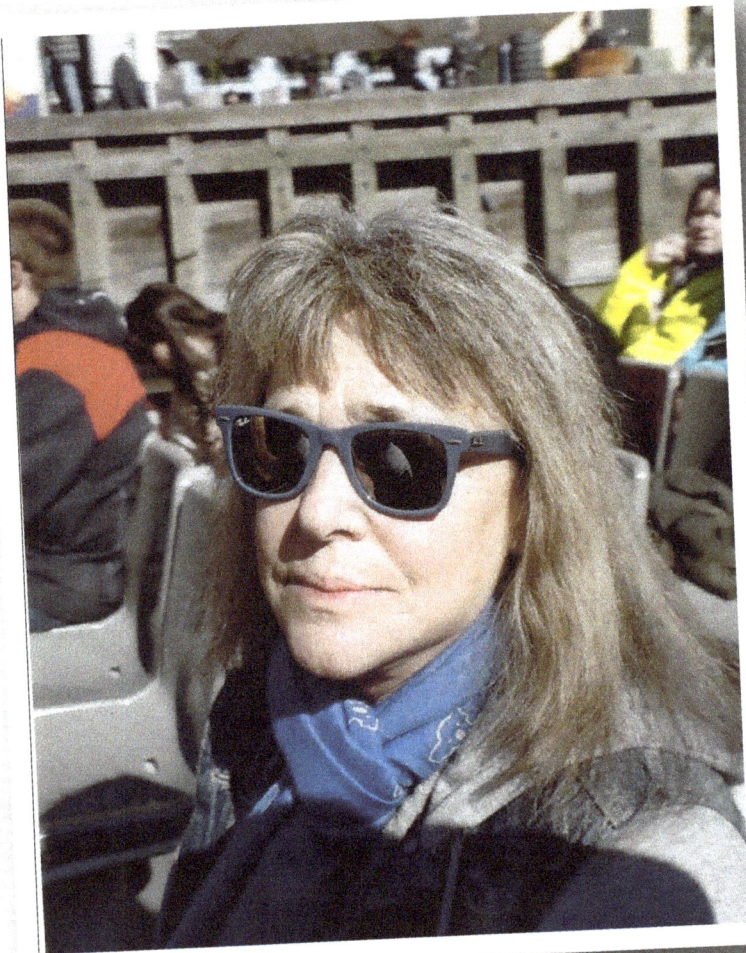

On a train, Germany, going to a gig, scarf for throat, sunglasses to sleep, could almost Be my 'down' time eh!!

This was written in the third person. I am one of those who others feel safe to discuss their problems. I always listen, am objective and non judgemental, and try and give good advice from my own wealth of life experience. I actually love helping people jump over the emotional hurdles in their lives.

Its' all doable folks, nothing stops you but 'you'.

Love Suzi

UNTIL MY MIND IS GONE

YOU HAUNT ME LATE AT NIGHT,
FLOATING ROUND IN MY ATMOSPHERE.
I NEED TO MAKE IT RIGHT,
TILL I KNOW THAT THIS SPACE IS CLEAR.
GET MY HEAD WHERE IT BELONGS
GRAB MY BAGGAGE, SO I CAN MOVE ON.

YOU KISSED ME ON MY LIPS.
WOUNDING ME DEEP INSIDE.
SOMETHING HAD TO GIVE.
I HAD NOWHERE ELSE TO HIDE.

YOU PUSHED ME TO THE EDGE
OF EMOTIONAL SUICIDE.
HANG THIS HEARTACHE OUT TO DRY
WIPE THESE TEARDROPS FROM MY EYE.

UNTIL MY MIND IS GONE, UNTIL MY MIND IS GONE.
GUESS I'LL JUST CARRY ON, UNTIL MY MIND IS GONE.

There is no better creation than mother nature
Photo credit Austen Burrows

In my past poetry books, I have included poems which became songs and songs which became poems and some which were both. There is no explanation for how this happens, just like there is no explanation for creativity. It happens. If you are a true 'artiste' you have no control. You just go with the flow. This next one was a song and got recorded as such, in preparation for my next solo album. It was decided during this 3 month period that we had somehow gotten lost and the songs were not what where we were heading. So, here are the lyrics. Now re-classified as poetry. I don't mind. It is what it is. But I do have 'demo's of these when they were songs... so who knows.. they may change status at a future date.

Never say never, as my mama used to say.

TRADING LICKS

(From a song to a poem, number 1)

COOL CAT CREEPING SIDEWALK STREAMING
MILK AND CREAMING
HIS TOWN UNTIL THE DAY BREAKS
ASPHALT PROWLING, ALLEY CAT HOWLING,
MEAN AND GROWLING,
HE KNOWS WHICH WAY THE STREET SHAKES

MIDNIGHT MOVER, JUNGLE GROOVER,
SWEET AND SMOOTHER.
WALKING ON THE WILD SIDE,
MOONLIT POTION, DEADLY MOTION
DANGEROUS NOTION,
HIS MIND IS ON THE BACK SLIDE.

TRADING LICKS, GET YOUR KICKS
MAKE IT CRUEL AND MAKE IT QUICK
SNIFFING 'ROUND, HUNTING DOWN
SILENT PAWS, DON'T MAKE A SOUND
YOU AIN'T NOTHING BUT A COOOOOOL CAT

COOL CAT CREEPING, PAVEMENT STEAMING
ASPHALT DREAMING
HE'S STALKING ON THE WILD SIDE,
MOONLIT NOTION, MIDNIGHT POTION
BAD, IN MOTION
SCRATCHING UP THE BACK SLIDE.

One of my rare moments 'off' bass guitar, probably doing an 'Otis Redding' song. 1966.

WHAT THE HELL

(From a song to a poem, number 2)

IF TRUTH IS JUST PERCEPTION,
BELIEVE IN WHAT WE CHOOSE
IF LOVE'S A MISCONCEPTION
THEN I'M TELLING YA BABE,
WE AIN'T GOT NOTHING TO LOSE
FEELING SO CONNECTED
SUDDENLY IT'S WRONG
COMPLETELY UNEXPECTED
LET'S RIDE THIS RIDE, AND DON'T WORRY
UNTIL ONE OF US BLOWS A FUSE.
NEVER WANNA LIE TO YOU
BUT, HOW WE GONNA MAKE IT THROUGH?

THE ENDING IS NEAR
FACE IT, ADMIT IT
AND YET IT'S NOT CLEAR
SO, WHAT THE HELL WE GONNA DO

WORDS TRAPPED IN CONVERSATION,
DON'T MEAN EXACTLY WHAT THEY MEAN.
IF LOVE NEEDS NO EXPLANATION,
THEN I'M TELLING YOU BABE,
THERE'S STILL SOMETHING IN BETWEEN
FEELINGS UNDETECTED
TRIED TO PLAY ALONG
SUDDENLY REJECTED
LET'S HIDE BEHIND ROSE COLOURED GLASSES
UNTIL WE'RE BACK WHERE WE BELONG

WHAT THE HELL WE GONNA DO
WHAT THE HELL WE GONNA DO
NO MORE US, NO MORE ME AND YOU
WHAT THE HELL CAN WE DO?

Mickie and Chris Most, both of whom had a profound influence on my life. Missed every single day.

I awoke after falling asleep early, Dec 4th 2024, around 11 pm.. felt the uncontrollable urge to go downstairs to my typewriter and compose this. Didn't question it, just did it. It literally flew out from fingers to page. I printed it out and put it on my husband's laptop in his office to read when he woke up. This is about Mickie and Chris Most.

We took his daughter to lunch the next day in London.
I told her this story. She said to me, 'yesterday was the anniversary of my mother's death.' I had no idea.
File this under 'wow'. I miss them both so much.

WHO KNEW

FROM THE TENDER AGE OF 21,
NEW COUNTRY, NEW WORLD, NEW LIFE
MY SUBSTITUTE FATHER WHO TOOK A CHANCE,
AND MY GUARDIAN ANGEL, HIS WIFE.
WHO KNEW?

TWO GEMINIS, SO MUCH IN COMMON
WE LAUGHED, WE SHARED, WE TALKED
IT'S A GOOD THING MY MOON IS IN CAPRICORN,
HER AND I, WHAT A DISTANCE WE WALKED.
WHO KNEW?

MY GEMINI MENTOR LEFT LONG AGO
AS HE ALWAYS KNEW HE WOULD
MY CAPRICORN FRIEND PROTECTED ME
THE ONLY ONE THAT COULD.
WHO KNEW?

I WANT TO MAKE THIS TOAST TO HER
HER PASSING STILL MAKES ME SAD,
SUCH A SPECIAL WOMAN OF MANY SHADES,
SHE WAS THE BEST FRIEND I EVER HAD.
WHO KNEW?

My heart, my soul, my home, where the family were raised.

(Continuing with songs that became poems instead, this next one was written intending to record it with my sisters and brother, but it didn't come to fruition, and the words are simply too good to waste.)

THE FAMILY TREE

(From a song to a poem)

THE FAMILY TREE OUR ROOTS RUN DEEP
ONE HEART, ONE SOUL, ITS TRUTH WE ALL SEEK
TOGETHER WE STAND
OUR BRANCHES CAN BEND.

MOTHER'S HEART, KEEPS THE BEAT
THIS FAMILY TREE, THERE WILL BE NO DEFEAT
TOGETHER WE BEND
TOGETHER WE MEND

ONE HEART, ONE SOUL
ONE HEART, ONE SOUL
ONE HEART, ONE SOUL
ONE HEART, ONE SOUL

ENCASED IN GOLDEN MEMORIES
LOST IN SPACE, SWEET MELODIES
ON OUR KNEES
LOVE'S SYMPHONY

STRIDE THROUGH THE YEARS, FIND YOUR VOICE
BRANCHES SPREAD, THEY HAVE NO CHOICE
TOGETHER WE STAND
HAND IN HAND

ONE HEART, ONE SOUL
ONE HEART, ONE SOUL
ONE HEART, ONE SOUL
DON'T EVER LET GO.

Australia, RHST, Robin Van Zandt lead singer Cheap Trick, note t-shirt, respect.

Another 'family' orientated musings, a poem, then a song, then a poem, back and forth.

Ping pong anyone?

IT'S A SHAKE DOWN MAMA

BLOOD TIES, AIN'T NO ESCAPING IT,
BLOOD LIES, AIN'T NO MISTAKING IT.
DON'T DROWN IN THE MISERY,
OF THEIR DISLOYAL SKULLDUGERY,
BLOOD BINDS LIKE A CHAIN, NO BREAKING IT.

ACCUSATIONS, JUST SWALLOW IT,
IMPLICATIONS, YOU'VE COME TO EXPECT IT.
YOU WALLOW IN THEIR FANTASY,
THEIR IMAGINED TREACHERY,
INCRIMINATIONS, BLAME, JUST DEFLECT IT

IT'S A BREAK DOWN MAMA, ITS CIRCUMSTANCE
IT'S A SHAKE DOWN MAMA, SUCH A DIRTY DANCE
TRAPPED IN THE NORMAL OF NON-NORMALITY
WRAPPED IN THEIR TRAP OF FALSE ANXIETY,
BLOOD TIGHTENS LIKE A NOOSE, TILL THEY HANG ON IT.

YES, IT'S A SHAKE DOWN MAMA, SO FEEL THAT GROOVE
NOT A BREAK DOWN MAMA, SO GET UP AND MOVE
YOU GOT A FIGHTING CHANCE TO END THIS THIS TRAGEDY
TO BE MORE THAN JUST ANOTHER SAD CASUALTY.
BLOOD TIES, BLOOD LIKES, NO MISTAKING.

SUZI QUATRO

W: www.suziquatro.com

Hard to tell the year, but in the nineties for sure, looks like after the bass solo to me.

There is actually an existing demo of this one. I love it, but again, not the direction this new album is heading in. This does not have a 'different' version, I have used the lyrics as written and called it a poem, no rhyme or reason.

I'D RATHER BE HEARD

(From a song to a poem)

SHOULD I TOUGHEN UP AND HIDE MY FEARS
ILLUSION, CONFUSION, THESE UNSHED TEARS
I'VE HAD ENOUGH OF STANDING SMALL
THE CHILL BREAKS MY WILL, YOUR FROZEN WALL

DON'T TRY TO CLIP MY WINGS, CAN'T KEEP ME DOWN
IT'S NOT YOUR SONG TO SING, SO DON'T MAKE A SOUND
WON'T GIVE UP MY RIGHT TO BE ME.
WON'T GIVE UP MY RIGHT TO FLY FREE.

I CAN'T RUN AWAY FROM MY HEART'S DESIRE
SO INTENSE, MY DEFENCES, THEY LIGHT MY FIRE
YOU CAN'T BURY 'ME', INSIDE 'YOUR' NEED
RESENTMENT LEAVES YOU NEVER, A MONSTER YOU FEED.

STRONG ENOUGH TO SHOW MY WEAKNESS
TO STAND UP EACH TIME I FALL
STRONG ENOUGH TO KNOW, I AM WHO I AM
AND I GIVE YOU MY WORD,
I'D RATHER BE HEARD

FLY AWAY ON WOUNDED WINGS
THIS SHADOW YOU CAST, IN THE PAST, BUT MEMORY CLINGS
TAKE YOUR PETTY LIES AND ANGRY SOUL
JEALOUSY BURNS, KARMA RETURNS, IT WILL LAY YOU LOW.

STRONG ENOUGH TO SHOW MY WEAKNESS
TO STAND UP EACH TIME I FALL
STRONG ENOUGH TO KNOW, I AM WHO I AM
AND I GIVE YOU MY WORD
I'D RATHER BE HEARD

Red Hot Summer Tour, Australia...
one of the few times I could wear my jumpsuit.
Credit: Chelle Carr

I always have felt it, have always talked about it trying to explain it to people, that feeling going from the loving warmth on stage, down those few steps into the dark. It's the loneliest feeling in the world.

And although I never (golden rule) touch a drink when I am doing a gig, I want my glass of champagne in a chilled glass as soon as I get to my dressing room. The bubbles enable me to float back down and not crash. Finally, I wrote about it.

As the previous one, there is a demo to this too. This 'was' the direction we were heading, but didn't make the cut.

Doesn't matter, it exists for the ears,

And for the mind.

DEAD ZONE

(From a song to a poem)

SCREAMING AND CRYING THE FOOTLIGHTS ARE SHINING,
HEART KEEPS A BEATING MY FINGERS ARE FLYING
MELT IN THE HEAT AS MY LEATHER IS FRYING, AND THEN
IT'S THE DEAD ZONE

OUTTA MY MIND LEAVING NORMAL BEHIND
FLOAT IN THE CLOUDS AND I PLAY WITH THE CROWDS
INTO THE LOUD YES, MY MOJO IS PROUD AND THEN
IT'S THE DEAD ZONE

SPOTLIGHT, LIGHT ME, DANCING IN ECSTACY
SWINGING SWAYING, CAUGHT UP IN FANTASY.
STAGE DOOR, TRAP DOOR, LOST AND FOUND
MY DESTINY

IT'S THE DEAD ZONE
I WALK THIS WALK ALONE
IT'S THE DEAD ZONE
NO DIRECTION KNOWN
THE ONLY PLACE TO GO
THE ONLY SPACE I KNOW
IT'S THE DEAD ZONE.........LOOK OUT I'M FALLING

SPITTING AND STOMPING MY BASS LINE IS STEAMING
SMILING AND SCREAMING, ANOTHER DAY DYING
SWIGGING AND SWEATING, MY BACKBONE IS ACHING AND THEN
IT'S THE DEAD ZONE

OUTTA MY MIND GUESS ITS NEARLY THAT TIME
I STOMP OFF THE STAGE, LEAVE MY EGO BEHIND
STAND IN MY FEAR, TILL I HEAR WHAT I NEED TO HEAR,
THEN, HERE I GO AGAIN.

This next one is interesting, a beautiful song in 3 movements, we all loved it, then it got put on the shelf, 'not suzi, not organic, and again, not where we're heading on this album, and again, there is a demo of it and I would be lying if I didn't say that I hope in the future we 'will' use it as the song it started life as.

In the meantime, enjoy the words.

*My mother. My heart, My rock, My moral compass,
My life.*

OH MAMA

(From a song to a poem, but still a song!)

ANY WAY THE WIND BLOWS
YOU'RE ALWAYS ON MY MIND.
LOOKING THROUGH THE WINDOW
MEMORY TRAPPED IN TIME.
I CAN SEE THAT PINK ROSE,
THE ONE YOU LEFT BEHIND.
I CAN HEAR YOUR HEARTBEAT,
THE FEELING IS SUBLIME.

OH MAMA, CAN'T YOU HEAR ME CALLING
OH MAMA, CAN'T YOU STOP ME FALLING
OH MAMA, OH MAMA, OH MAMA
SINCE THAT DAY YOU LEFT ME,
YOU'RE NEVER FAR AWAY
EVERY ROAD I'VE TRAVELLED,
YOU'VE SHOWED ME THE WAY
YOU'D SAID THERE WOULD BE A LITTLE HEARTACHE
SEASONED WITH SOME SMILES.
JUST TO FEEL YOUR TOUCH AGAIN,
I'D WALK A MILLION MILES.

OH, MAMA CAN'T YOU HEAR ME CALLING
OH, MAMA CAN'T YOU STOP ME FALLING
OH, MAMA OH MAMA OH MAMA.

DON'T YOU BLAME ME, YOU CAN'T REARRANGE ME
I'LL BE ALL THAT I SHOULD BE, AS LONG AS YOU LET ME.
DON'T YOU SHAME, ME, NO ONE CAN CHANGE ME
I AM WHO I SHOULD BE, SO LONG AS YOU ACCEPT ME.

YOU NEVER SAW ME STANDING THERE
I WAS YOUR STRENGTH; I WAS YOUR ANGEL IN DISPAIR
I CAN HEAR YOU CALLING
REACH TO THE SKY, I'M SHINING THERE
DEEP IN YOUR HEART, DEEP IN YOUR SOUL, THIS LOVE I SHARE
I CAN HEAR YOU CALLING, I CAN STOP YOU FALLING DOWN.

OH, MAMA CAN'T YOU HEAR ME CALLING
OH, MAMA CAN'T YOU STOP ME FALLING
OH, MAMA, OH MAMA, OH MAMA

Innsbruck, Austria, on the road, finding a moment to capture the moment. It was a 'snap' decision.

(I had this title for years and years, tried various ways of working it in the a song on various instruments, and finally realizing, it is not a song it is a poem, lyrically speaking.)

ROSES AND ALIBIS

(From a song to a poem)

I WOULD HAVE PREFERRED THE DREAM,
SO, SPARE ME THIS CLOSING SCENE.
YOU TOLD HER THAT YOU WERE FREE,
EXACTLY WHAT YOU TOLD ME!
SO HOW DO YOU SLEEP AT NIGHT?
PLAYING US BOTH, GOD KNOWS IT'S NOT RIGHT.

AS OUR LOVED GROWS COLD
I WATCH THE TRUTH UNFOLD
INTO MY FEARS I FALL
BUT I COME OUT THE OTHER SIDE, STANDING TALL
NEVER A FOOL AM I
AND BELIEVE ME, I WON'T CRY.

ROSES AND ALIBIS,
I DON'T WANT YOUR LITTLE WHITE LIES, ANYMORE.
ROSES AND ALIBIS,
I DON'T' NEED YOUR LITTLE WHITE LIES, ANYMORE.
SO TAKE YOUR ROSES AND ALIBIS
AND FFFFFF....LY AWAY.

TRUE AS A HEART CAN BE
THE TWO OF US, SWEET HARMONY?
BUT YOU'RE LIVING YOUR FANTASY,
AND THE THREE OF US, IS ONE TOO MUCH, FOR ME.
SO HOW DO YOU SLEEP AT NIGHT?
PLAYING US BOTH, GOD KNOWS, IT'S NOT RIGHT.

ROSES AND ALIBIS,
I DON'T WANT YOUR LITTLE WHITE LIES, ANYMORE.
ROSES AND ALIBIS,
I DON'T' NEED YOUR LITTLE WHITE LIES, ANYMORE.
SO TAKE YOUR ROSES AND ALIBIS
AND FFFFFF....LY AWAY.

Met so many artists on the road, too many to count, this is one of my favourite girls, RHS, Australia, Baby Animals lead singer Suze Demarchi.. just love her. Such a pretty girl, inside and out.

LET ME SHINE
(poem that stayed a poem)

SOMETIMES I WANT TO RUN AND HIDE,
THOSE LIES EMOTIONAL SUICIDE
TILL I'M ALL UNDONE
RIGHT OR WRONG
I WON'T BELONG TO ANYONE
MY VISION,
MY FIGHT,
MY LIFE.

COMPROMISE, A COMMON GROUND?
SAY 'I DO', THEN TWIST IT AROUND.
BLACK AND BLUE, NOTHING NEW IN INHUMANITUY
LOST AND FOUND? GUESS THAT'S LOVE'S DICHOMOTY.
MY MOVIE,
MY LIGHT
MY LIFE.

WHOEVER I AM
WHATEVER I DO
LET IT BE 'ME'
LET IT BE 'MINE',
LET 'ME' SHINE

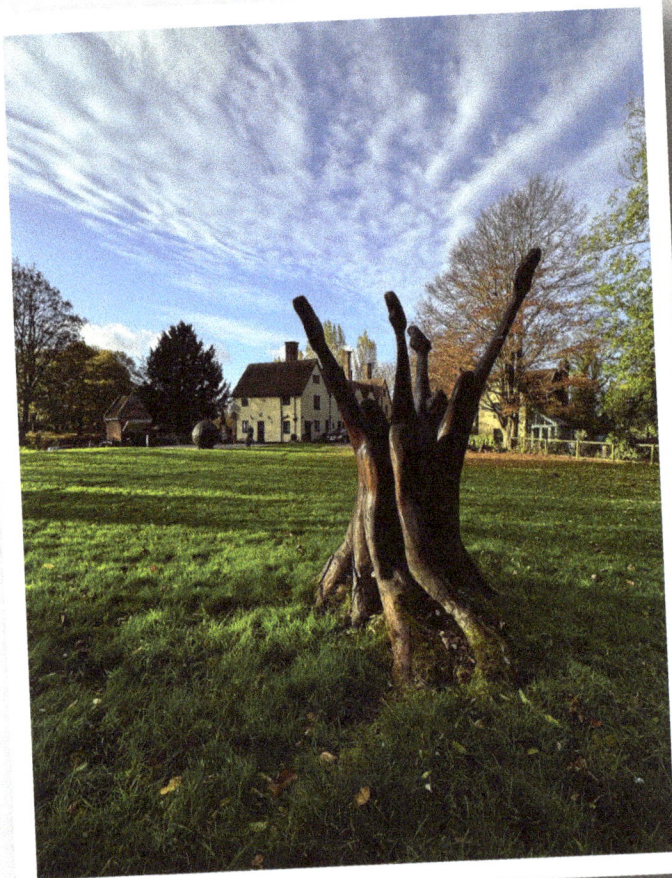

During the isolation of Covid, I had this view to inspire me.
Credit: Neville Cooper

This next one goes in the same category with 'oh mama'.. demos and loved by me big time, but again, didn't go along with the musical vision we were creating for my next solo album, mid-way through at the time of assembling this book, and again, I do hope this will be included on a future album. And again, in the meantime, enjoy the words. I really, truly do love what this says, it's the Dylan in me emerging. (ps. I LOVE this as a song) No mistake it was written during the covid lockdown.

THE OTHER SIDE OF CRAZY
(from a song to a poem)

THE OTHER SIDE OF CRAZY, TRAPPED INSIDE INSANITY,
YOU WAKE UP IN THE SHADOWS, BROKEN DREAMS AND MEMORIES
YOU REALISE YOU NEVER KNEW, HOW LONELY THIS WORLD COULD BE,
THEN YOU REACH OUT YOUR LOVING ARMS,
AND HUG THE GHOST OF LOVE BETWEEN.

THE DANCE FLOOR IS EMPTY, CAN'T SELL TICKETS AT THE DOOR.
A CIGARETTE, A SHOT OF WHISKEY, NOTHING MATTERS ANYMORE.
PHILOSOPHISE, TILL THE SUN GOES DOWN, ANALYZE MY MORAL CODE
CONTEMPLATE MY NAVEL, BUT THE MEANING DIES,
DOWN THIS DEAD-END ROAD

WE'RE ON THE OTHER SIDE OF CRAZY
BEYOND THE OTHER SIDE OF UNSCRIPTED REALITY
I'LL PLAY THE GAME UNTIL THE WHEEL STOPS SPINNING AROUND
I'LL GAMBLE THE ODDS, LIFE'S A GAME OF ROULETTE
BUT I NEVER WILL FORGET, THE OTHER SIDE OF CRAZY

WE'RE ON THE OTHER SIDE OF CRAZY,
NO BEYOND, THE OTHER SIDE OF SUSPENDED REALITY.
I'LL PLAY THE GAME, UNTIL THE WHEEL STOPS SPINNING AROUND.
I'LL GAMBLE THE ODDS, IN THE GAME OF ROULETTE,
I'LL GAMBLE MY CHANCES, I'LL LAY DOWN A BET,
WINNER OR LOOSER, I'LL HAVE NO REGRET
CUZ I NEVER, I NEVER CAN FORGET,
THE OTHER SIDE OF CRAZY.

Me, attitude on show, Alan Ballad, sadly missed. He 'got' me'.

(Seems to be a recurring theme, or is it a recurring dream, works either way, or is it obscure and in between?)

FOREVER BURN

LIFE WITHOUT YOU,
IT'S BEEN IMPOSSIBLE TO DO
I'M SO LOST INSIDE THIS PLACE
EMPTY THOUGHTS, EMPTY SPACE.
LIKE A THIEF IN THE NIGHT
YOU STEAM MY DREAMS, BLOCK MY LIGHT,
I ESCAPE INSIDE MY MIND,
WHERE I SEE CLEARLY, LOVE IS BLIND

ROMANCE IS BLUE
A LEAST IT IS, WHEN IT'S WITH YOU
THOSE FLAMES THAT YOU IGNITE,
NO MORE WILL, NO MORE FIGHT
I JUST CAN'T SAY GOODBYE
WITHIN LUST, A GIRL CAN DIE,
CAN'T FIND THE STRENGTH TO WALK AWAY
IT MAY KILL ME, BUT I'LL STAY

FOREVER BURN, FOREVER BURN
INTO THE FIRE, ALL THAT YOU'VE LEARNED
FOREVER BURN, FOREVER BURN
DROWN IN THE MIRE, THE FATE YOU'VE EARNED

*I don't know what I would do if I could not do this anymore.
It is the air I breathe.*

3 a.m. thoughts are destined to wake you no matter how soundly you sleep. It's when your daytime' face is off.
Your defenses are down. Alone in bed praying to whatever God you pray to. Asking for guidance, help, forgiveness, salvation, reciting the words you learned as a child, hoping they will bring you comfort, like your mother's smile used to do.

SLEEP

Dated May 10th, 2024, 01:18

SLEEPTIME DISRUPTED WITH AGEING THOUGHTS
A DILEMMA WITH NO ANSWER
LACED WITH BEGETS AND BEGOTS
NOTHING LEFT, NO TREASURE

YOU HAVE NO WAY TO MEASURE
THIS UNSETTLED STATE OF MIND.
I HOPE GOD KEEPS A LEDGER,
OF ALL YOU'VE LEFT BEHIND.

HAVE I DONE MY BEST? WHO KNOWS.
WHAT ACCIDENTS HAVE I CAUSED?
HAVE I WOUNDED THE ONES I LOST MOST?
THESE THOUGHTS GIVE ME REASON TO PAUSE.

THERE COMES A TIME IN ONE'S LIFE
WHEN NOTHING REALLY MATTERS.
ALL PARTIES SHOULD COME TOGETHER
AND LEAVE THE CRAZY, FOR THE MAD HATTERS

SLEEP ELUDES TONIGHT
POETRY REARS ITS HEAD.
AND NOW I HAVE TYPED THIS LAST ONE,
I'LL TIP TOE UP TO BED

(typing this out on Nov 30th, 17:12, no change on the above)

Onstage, Australia. The song remains the same.
Credit, Julie Ainsworth.

As I am typing all these poems out for poetry book volume 3, 'Through My Pain', doing a little each day, there is an emerging pattern of bravado/sensitivity, bravery/ cowardice, cunning/ naivity/happiness/sorrow. Can all these be me?

Apparently, so. Well, I am a Gemini, not an excuse (maybe a little), just a fact of life.

And so say all of us!!!!

I CRY ALONE

SO MANY DREAMS HAVE BEEN LOST ,
TOO MANY LIES HAVE BEEN TOLD.
NOW IT SEEMS THAT THE COST
IS TO CARRY THAT LOAD.
I WON'T CARRY THIS LOAD NO MORE.
TOO MANY SEASONS HAVE GONE.
YES, THE DIE'S BEEN CAST
CIRCUMSTANCES, MISSED CHANCES,
ALL IN THE PAST,
AND I WON'T CARRY THAT PAST NO MORE.

ALL EXPOSED IT'S NOT PRETTY
A ONE-WAY STREET MOST OF MY LIFE
FEELING ASHAMED OF SELF PITY,
BUT BLOOD IS THICKER THAN THE RIVER I CRY

FOREVER SEARCHING
A JOURNEY WITHOUT AN END.
HERE'S TO ENEMIES' MAS-A- QUER-RAIDING AS FRIENDS
I WON'T CARRY THESE FRIENDS NO MORE
ALL THESE YEARS I'VE BEEN BURNING
INSIDE THEIR PRECIOUS GAME,
LOOK INTO YOUR SOULS,
YOU'LL SEE 'YOU'RE' TO BLAME.
AND, I WON'T CARRY THAT BLAME NO MORE

SO, I CRY ALONE I CRY ALONE
I CRY ALONE AND ONE DAY I'LL DIE ALONE
I'LL TWIST THIS TALE OF FLESH AND BONE,
EAT IT UP, SPIT IT OUT TO THE GROUND,
THEN BURY MY PAIN WITHOUT A SOUND
I CRY ALONE, I WILL ALWAYS CRY ALONE.

Me and Cyril, Stumblin' In

HOT AIR BALLOON

WANNA TAKE A RIDE TO THE SKY?
WANNA UNTIE THE TETHERED ROPES?
IN A WICKER BASKET WITH SIDES HIGH,
WANNA DRIFT OVER THE SLOPES?

SEE THE CLOUDS ACCUMULATING,
SEE THE STORM DRAWING NEARBY,
YOU APPROACH, HESITATING,
IS IT THE HEIGHT THAT YOU FEAR, WHY?

ONCE YOUR UP AND SOARING,
YOU RELINQUISH YOUR CONTROL.
WHICH DIRECTION, THERE'S NO WARNING,
AT THE MERCY OF THE WINDS THAT BLOW.

DO YOU LEAP IN THAT HOT AIR BALLOON,
OR DO YOU DIG YOUR HEELS IN THE GROUND?
CAN YOU JOURNEY THROUGH THIS STORM
OR WILL YOU FLOUNDER, JUMP, DROWN.

A LEAP OF FAITH IS REQUIRED,
HOLDING ONTO THAT FEELING CALLED LOVE.
THIS HOT AIR BALLOON OF MEMORIES,
CAN IT FLY YOU HIGH ABOVE?

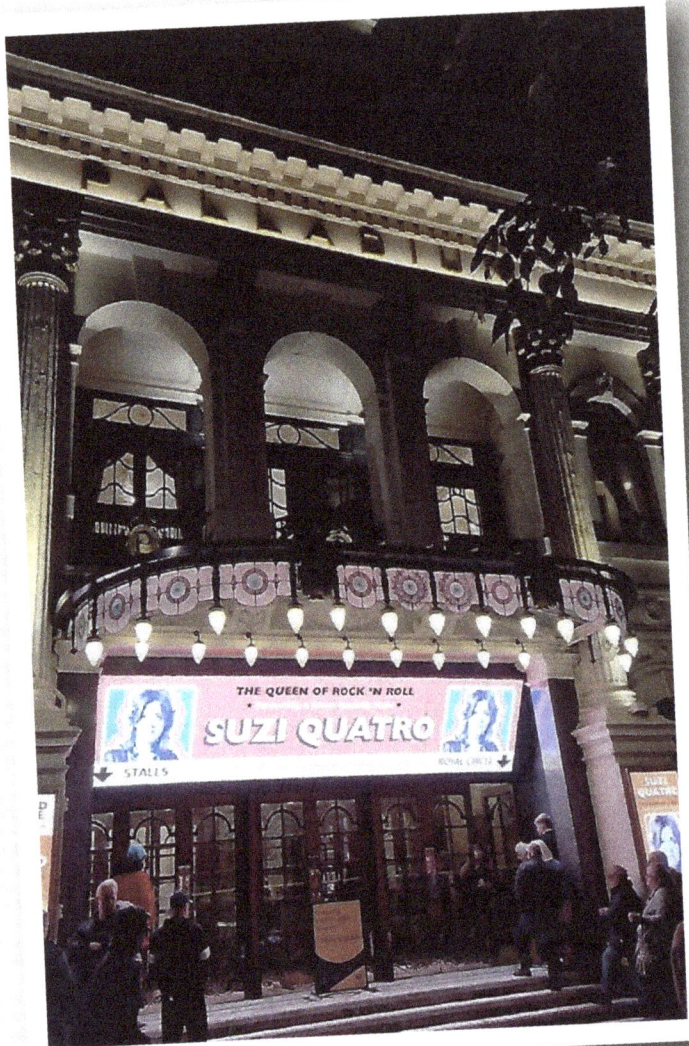

Royal Albert Hall, my name up in lights... what a moment.

Oh boy was I angry when I wrote this. A certain person who I shall 'not' name, who doesn't like me at all, never has, has no time for me, never did, actually had the nerve to ask me for money when she was down and out. Not even first hand, through somebody else. If she had asked me directly I would have respected her more, but the answer would still be no.

I have a demo of this but decided it is too negative to set to music. She doesn't deserve it.

HAND OUT

YOUR MIND IS DIRTY, ON YOUR SIDE OF THE STREET,
LET THE VERBAL ABUSE BEGIN.
YOU LOVE TO HATE ME, EVERY CHANCE THAT YOU GET,
KARMA'S KICKING YOU DOWN AGAIN.
YOU'RE WAITING OUTSIDE MY DOOR,
SO, WHAT IS IT YOU'RE WAITING FOR?
YOUR WORDS ARE UGLY, YOUR INTENTIONS ARE CRUEL,
AS YOU SHOOT TO KILL THE BEAST.
YOUR HEART IS HUNGRY, BUT IT'S EMPTY OF FUEL,
KISMET, BECOMES THE FEAST.
YOU'RE WAITING OUTSIDE MY DOOR,
SO, WHAT IS IT YOU'RE WAITNG FOR?
POISON ARROWS, LIKE TOXIC WASTE
NO POINT WILL HIT ITS MARK.
ACCUSATIONS, LEAVE A BITTER TASTE
THERE IS NO LIGHT INSIDE YOUR DOOR.
YOU'RE WAITING OUTSIDE MY DOOR,
SO, WHAT IS IT YOU'RE WAITING FOR?
LOOK ME STRAIGHT IN THE EYE,
CAN YOU POSSIBLY TELL ME WHY?
REVENGE IS NOT SO SWEET,
NOT WHEN TWO DESTINIES MEET.

HAND OUT, ONLY CASH DESIRED,
HAND OUT NO INTEGRITY REQUIRED
HAND OUT, YOU'RE STANDING SO SMALL,
LIES, YOUR LIES, YOUR DIRTY LITTLE LIES
HYPOCRISY MUST FALL, THAT'S ALL.
SO PUT YOUR HAND OUT, THEN DO IT AGAIN.
IT'S THE ONE HAND, YOU WILL NEVER WIN.

Pleasure Seekers, Original line-up, 1964

Once in the *Pleasure Seekers*, around 1969, we were travelling through the *Everglades* at night and we ran out of gas.

We were stranded there, not daring to step outside and get eaten by alligators. We were there all night, and it gave me a life-long fear of running on empty.

OUT OF GAS

SPLUTTER, JERK, STOP, YOU RUN OUT OF FUEL,
AND SUDDER TO A HALT WITH AN EMPTY TANK.
DO YOU TRY, BUT CAN'T PLAY ANY MUSIC?
DO YOU SHIVER, BUT CAN'T TURN ON THE HEAT
ARE YOU COLD, HELPESS AND TIRED?
GUESS YOU'RE STRANDED ON THE HIGHWAY OF LIFE
GUESS YOU ARE................. OUT OF GAS!

THE MILES TRAVELLED BEHIND YOU,
THE STORMS WEATHERED, TRAPPED IN TIME,
OUTDATED BOUNDARIES 'TWIXT YOU TWO,
PASSIONATE HATRED, THE PERFECT CRIME?
ON THAT GROUND YOU WALKED IN FAITH
NOW SUNK IN QUICKSAND, IMPOSSIBLE TO CLIMB.

THERE ARE NO STATIONS IN SIGHT,
NO OASIS TO EASE YOUR PLIGHT.
SETTLING IN FOR AN EMPTY NIGHT.
NOBODYS' WRONG AND NOBODY'S RIGHT
FUTURE IN THE BALANCE, STOP OR GO?
EXAMINE THE CHALLENGE, YES.... OR NO?
DESTINATION ZERO, GUESS YOU ARE.... OUT OF GAS.

IN THE TWILIGHT HOURS, YOU COMPOSE
NO NOISE TO OBSCURE 'YOUR' TRUTH
YOURS IS ONLY ONE SIDE OF THE EQUATION,
BUT BALANCE OWNS HALF THE PROOF.
STRANDED ON THE HIGHWAY OF LOVE
NO ESCAPE, ALL MUST COME TO PASS
GUESS YOU BOTH ARE....... OUT OF GAS.

Celebration Service
for the life of

Andrew Maurice Dowding

23rd July 1961 - 7th August 2023

62 years

Andy Dowding, with me for many years, cried my eyes out when he was called to join that big band in the sky. Missed big time.

Sometimes I think about what happens we you do indeed let it go. I am convinced there is a moment of decision, and then whoosh... up to the spirit in the sky.

I have lost many musicians who I have either been in a band with or they have played in mine after I went solo.

To all those souls I say thank you, bless you and R.I.P.

We'll meet again.

WHAT HAPPENS?

WHAT HAPPENS WHEN YOU LET IT ALL GO?
THOSE DREAMS FULL OF LOSSES,
THOSE SCHEMES NAILED TO THEIR CROSSES,
WHAT HAPPENS WHEN YOU CLOSE THE SHOW?

WHAT HAPPENS WHEN YOU LET IT ALL GO?
THOSE FANTASIES OF FLAMING DESIRES
DISCARDED NEEDS, BURNING IN FIRES
WHAT HAPPENS WHEN YOU SINK SO LOW?

WHAT HAPPENS WHEN YOU LET IT ALL GO?
WHEN BOTTOM FEELS JUST LIKE THE TOP.
WHEN A HIT SMELLS THE SAME AS A FLOP.
WHAT HAPPENS IN THAT JOURNEY BELOW?

WHAT HAPPENS WHEN YOU LET IT ALL GO?
WHAT HAPPENS WHEN YOU LET IT ALL GO?
IT'S CURTAINS WHICHEVER WAY YOU GO.
GUESS IT'S TIME TO CLOSE THIS SHOW.

A Service to Celebrate the Life
of
Dave Neal
24th April 1952 ~ 20th November 2020

Thanet Crematorium
Friday 11th December 2020
1:00 p.m.

Also sadly passed. We were like brother and sister.
Never was there a better combination of bass player
and drummer, (Excepting The Funk Brothers).
His kit now sits in my home studio. How magic is that.
Rip.xxx

FRIENDSHIP. A TWO WAY STREET?

DO YOU SET THE BAR WAY TOO HIGH
OF WHAT A TRUE FRIEND SHOULD BE?
DO YOUR EXPECTATIONS DENY,
A SONG SUNG IN HARMONY?

DO YOU LISTEN WITH YOUR HEART,
WHEN THEY SHARE THEIR TALES OF WOE.
OR ONLY LISTEN WITH YOUR EARS,
FAKES TEARS, ALL PART OF THE SHOW.

AND IF YOUR BAR IS TOO HIGH,
FOR ANYONE TO JUMP OVER IT.
MUST THEY LEARN THEN HOW TO LIMBO,
DANCE 'YOUR' DANCE, OR LUMP IT.

WHAT KIND OF A FRIEND ARE YOU?
DO YOU FALSELY ACCUSE.
'WHERE WERE YOU WHEN I NEEDED YOU'?
THEN STEP BACK AND LIGHT THE FUSE.

OR IS YOUR COLOUR YELLOW
AFRAID TO SPEAK YOUR MIND.
IN FEAR OF LOSING A FRIENDSHIP
THAT WAS NEVER 'YOUR' DESIGN.

TRUE FRIENDSHIP IS A GIVE AND TAKE,
TRUE FRIENDSHIP IS HARD TO BEAT.
TRUE FRIENDSHIP IS IMPOSSIBLE TO FAKE.
TRUE FRIENDSHIP, A TWO WAY STREET.

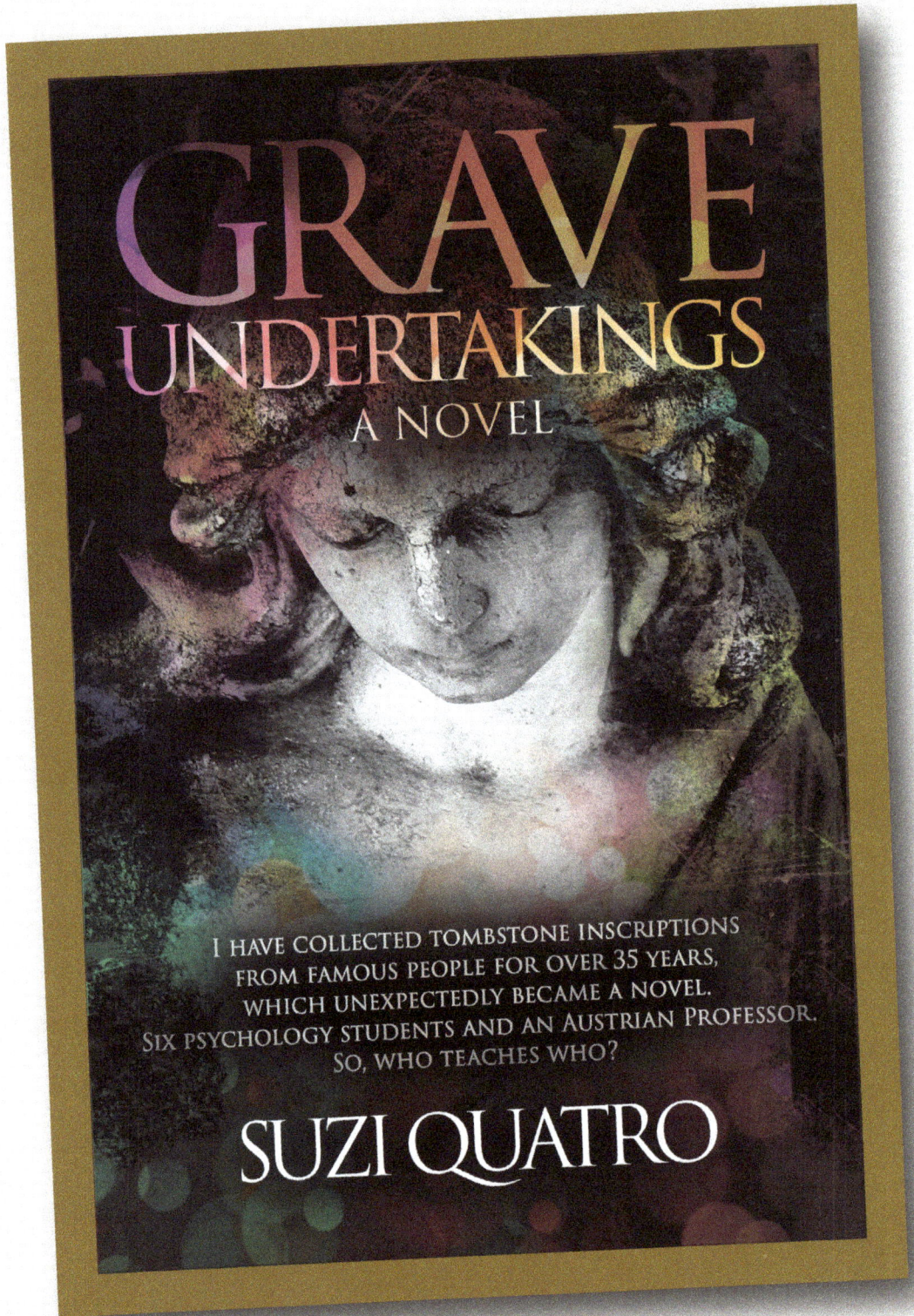

My second novel , 7th book, released April 17, 2025. Touching you, touching me and eventually touching every single one of us.

THE END

THERE IS NO RIGHT WAY, THERE IS NO WRONG,
THERE IS NO SAFE WAY, NO SHORT, NOR LONG.
NO LAME EXCUSES FOR BAD DECISIONS,
IT PART OF 'YOUR' PLAN, 'YOUR' LIFE'S COLLISIONS.

YOU PAINTED YOUR DREAM WITH VIBRANT COLOURS,
YOU PLANNED AND SCHEMED, UNDER THE COVERS.
AFRAID TO REACH THOSE DIZZY HEIGHTS,
AFRAID TO FAIL AND EXTINGUISH THE LIGHTS.

AND SO, YOU TRAVEL AND GO YOUR DISTANCE
WITH OPTIMISTIC PRAYERS OF BLIND PERSISTENCE.
NIGHT TIME BECKONS, THOUGHTS ARRIVE,
WILL I AWAKE, WILL I SURVIVE?

THE END IS THE END, IT COMES TO US ALL
ALL WE CAN HOPE FOR IS THE HIGH, BEFORE THE FALL.
THE END IS THE END, HOW MUCH TIME, I HEAR YOU SAY
UNTIL THE END MY FRIEND, AND WORDS HAVE DRIFTED AWAY

New boat in pond.
Credit Austen Burrows

How are you enjoying the journey so far? If you can swim, you will reach the other side. If you can't, then just enjoy the ride. Sit on your surfboard and wait for the will of the tide. Nature 'will' take it's course and so will 'you'

Nature, of course, or possibly, of coarse.
Works either way.

YOU AND ME

YES, HE IS GETTING OLDER,
AND THAT IS A FACT.
BUT NO MATTER HOW MEAN HE GETS,
HER HEART KNOWS IT'S ONLY AN ACT.

SHE FELL IN LOVE WITH HIM MANY YEARS AGO,
AND SHE LOVES HIM STILL
NO MATTER WHAT KNIVES HE THROWS,
HER LOVE HE CANNOT AND WILL NOT KILL.

SHE AND HE, WILL LAST THROUGH THE STORM.
SHE AND HE POETICALLY.
THIS IS WRITTEN FROM HER HEART,
SHE AND HE, MEANT TO BE.

I have always believed I was 'drawn' to this house by unseen forces. Been here since 1980 and there is no place on earth I would rather be. It is my peace in a world of madness. Long may it stand.

Photo Credit Austen Burrows

If it is correct that we choose which body to come into in each incarnation, in order to work out situations from past incarnations, then that would explain this next poem perfectly. I am spiritually minded, and do believe in reincarnation.

Have done since a child. I am a mere student in the 'school of life', and hope to graduate this time round. IN FACT, I have always been aware that this IS my last time round.

THE ARCHITECT
(never truer words were written)

AM I THE ARCHITECT OF YOUR DOWNFALL?

OR DO YOU SIMPLY NEED TO HATE ME
FOR YOUR LIFE TO MAKE SENSE?

JUST BECAUSE YOUR ENTRANCE WAS BLOCKED,
DOES NOT MEAN IT WAS LOCKED!

LOOK AT YOURSELF,
YOU HAVE THE KEY TO UNLOCK THE ANSWERS.

THE PEACE YOU ARE SEARCHING FOR
IS WITHIN YOUR GRASP.

IT IS UP TO YOU TO FIND IT.
UNLOCK YOUR HEART.

MINE HAS ALWAYS BEEN OPEN
MY WISH IS, YOU HAVE AWOKEN

YOU ARE THE ARCHITECT OF YOUR DOWNFALL.

IF YOU NEED TO HATE ME THEN SO BE IT
I KNOW THE TRUTH, AND I SEE IT.

I AM NOT THE ARCHITECT OF YOUR DOWNFALL
I AM THE ONE WHO LOVED YOU,
ON THE OTHER SIDE OF YOUR WALL.

A big daddy hug with our children.

(I am my mother's daughter and this poem proves it)

UNITE THE PLAYERS

CAN WE UNITE THE PLAYERS,
IDENTIFY THE GOOD AND THE BAD?
THOSE SLIPPERY SERPENTS, THOSE GAME PLAYERS.
DOOM MERCHANTS AND SOOTH SAYERS.
ALL GETTING EQUAL TIME,
WITH THIS TAPESTRY OF CARPET LAYERS,
THE WORLD CAN BE AN UGLY PLACE,
FULL OF USERS, ABUSERS AND FAKERS.
IT'S HARD TO FIND THE GOLD,
ITS HARD TO BE A DREAM MAKER
IF WE CAN UNITE THE PLAYERS,
THE NASTY, THOSE CRUEL BALL BREAKERS.
CAN WE CREATE A PERFECT SPACE
OF KIND DECENCY, LIFE SHAPERS,
OR DESTINED TO MERELY EXIST,
ALONGSIDE MURKEY BACKSTREET TRAITORS.
CAN WE UNITE THE PLAYERS
THESE EVIL PEOPLE HATERS.
IF WE UNITE THESE PLAYERS
GLOOM MERCHANTS AND SOUL TRADERS,
SEPARATE THE GOOD FROM THE BAD,
CAN WE PUT A STOP TO THESE TOMB RAIDERS.
SEPARATE THE GOOD FROM THE BAD,
MAYBE STOP THESE EVIL INVADERS.
TURN THE GLOOM AND THE DOOM INTO 'GLAD',
HEAR YE, HEAR YE, CALLING ONE AND ALL
UNITE THE PLAYERS, HEAR THE CALL.
UNITE THE PLAYERS, SAVE US ALL.

How beautiful is this, and how peaceful. And....... Breathe.

Photo Credit Austen Burrows

Marvellous gig in Belfast, staying at hotel with Titanic memorablia, fascinating, simply fascinating and of course... sitting at the bar with my glass of chardonay, there was no way I could not write about what I was feeling.

Help! Woman overboard.

BELFAST

I FOUND MY FREEDOM IN BELFAST TONIGHT.
A FREEDOM I DIDN'T KNOW I WAS MISSING.
THE BUSY BARTENDER, THE FRANTIC WAITERS,
THRONGS OF PEOPLE YAPPING AWAY, DRINK AND CIGARETTES.
NOISEY SEALS IN CHOPPY WATERS,
THESE SOUNDS INVADED MY THOUGHTS.
I WAS SURROUNDED BY MODELS AND PAINTINGS
OF THE GRAND TITANIC THAT SANK.
I'VE BEEN SINKING A LONG TIME, WITH NO IDEA,
WATER HAS BEEN TRICKLING IN DROP BY DROP,
TONIGHT, I HIT THE ICEBERG, WITHOUT ANY WARNING.
SO, I GRABBED A PIECE OF WOOD
AND FLOATED BACK TO SAFETY,
ON WAVES OF AWARNESS OF WHO I AM,
GLAD TO BE ALIVE.
GOD BLESS THOSE WHO DIDN'T' MAKE IT
I FOUND MY FREEDOM IN BELFAST TONIGHT.

RHA/QSP....... Royal Albert Hall, Quatro, Scott and Powell... joined me on stage. What a great album we made.

Beside being fascinated with graveyards (Grave Undertakings), I am also fascinated with wandering around Casinos, especially the Crown in Melbourne. Many tours I have been there alone, in my special loft suite. I often go down and wander through, stopping and watching, observing the dance, but not taking part.

This is not the music I relate to.
But it does have its own 'rhythm'.

CASINO
(written Oct 31, 2022 at 22:23))

WANDERING THROUGH THIS MERRY GO ROUND
ONCE MAGNIFICENTLY OVERWHELMING.
NOW FULL OF BEEN THERE'S AND DONE THAT'S,
FALLS FLAT, SO LOW, UNDEMANDING

ROULETTE WHEELS SPINNING FRANTICLY AROUND,
FOOLISH FOOLS, PLACE A BET.
THREADBARE CARPETS OF BROKEN DREAMS,
THEY'RE ALL GAMBLING TO FORGET.

WHISKEY SOUR, MARTINI WITH A TWIST,
NEEDED TO NUMB THEIR LOSSES.
SHORT SKIRTED COCKTALK WAITRESSES,
BEND OVER, DELIVERING SAUCES.

WAGERING CRAZILY ON SO MANY NUMBERS,
DRINKS ON THE LEFT, CHIPS ON THE RIGHT.
COVERING ALL POSSIBLE SPACES,
NO LOGIC, NO WILL TO FIGHT.

IS BLACKJACK YOUR POISON, THE ACE, THE KING?
AS THE CROUPIER DEALS THE VERDICT.
YOU CAN'T RESIST, TAKING A HIT ON FIFTEEN!
THE RESULT IS PERFECTLY IMPERFECT.

AND THE WORST PART IS YOUR SITTING ON THE END,
ALL EYES BEGGING YOU TO RESIST.
BUT TEMPTATION PROVES TOO HARD TO QUASH
YOU TAKE THE BUST CARD, ANGRY CLENCHED FIST.

ONE ARMED BANDITS LINE THE FLOOR,
CRAMMED BETWEEN ZOMBOID FACES.
PUSHING AND PUSHING THAT BUTTON
CRAMMING COINS INTO EMPTY SPACES?

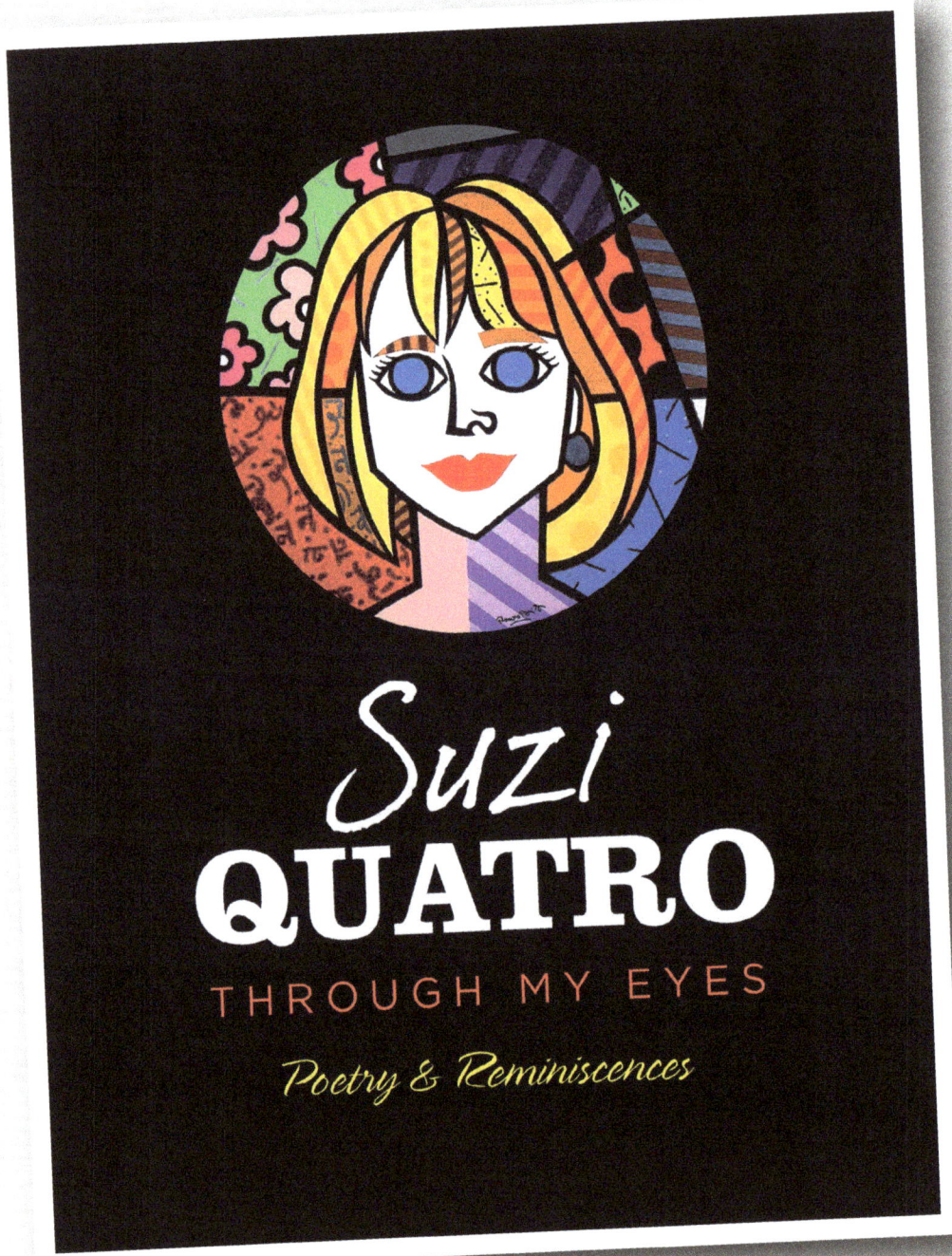

First poetry book where I attempt to explain how my heart, mind and soul work. Still haven't quite figured it out though. I just know I have to keep writing.

CASINO
(Continued)

DING DING DING, YOUR CASH DWINDLES DOWN,
BUT THE HOPE KEEPS YOU GOING.
TILL THE COINS IN YOUR POCKET RUN DRY
AND THE 'WIN' SIGN, NOT SHOWING.

WANDERING THROUGH THIS MERRY GO ROUND
AMBLING FROM TABLE TO TABLE
NOT TEMPTED TO PARTICIPATE
YOU SIMPLE WATCH THE DIS-ABLED

OBSERVING NOW FROM AFAR
TEMPTATION HAS BECOME A STRANGER
TO THROW YOUR MONEY AGAINST THE WALL IS
NO LONGER EVEN A REMOTE DANGER
IN THIS CASINO OF LIFE
YOU WILL WAGER NO MORE,
YOU'VE CASHED IN YOUR CHIPS,
YOU'VE EVENED THE SCORE,
HAND GESTURE.... NO MORE
BETS.

(phew.. must have been a looooooong walk)

Photo Credit Jess McGilwraith

Undoubtedly one of my favourite moments in the show. Have been singing this song since it was released.

As I say to the audience each night.. this is from my heart to your heart. And I mean it.

MOTHER'S DAY

THIS WAS ALWAYS A SPECIAL DAY FOR ME.
I WOULD SPEND MY ALLOWANCE HAPPILY,
ON A GIFT FOR MY MOTHER, WHO WAS, IN MY OPINION,
JUST THIS SIDE OF A SAINT ON EARTH.
SHE WOULD ALWAYS TELL ME,
DON'T WASTE YOUR MONEY ON PRESENTS FOR ME.
THIS WOULD HURT MY FEELINGS DEEPLY, BECAUSE,
I DIDN'T THINK IT WAS WASTED, AN IVORY COMB
A HAND PAINTED BREAD AND BUTTER SET, A BROACH,
NOTHING WAS WASTED ON THIS SPECIAL MOTHER,
WHO HAD LOVE, TIME AND UNDERSTANDING
FOR EVERY CHILD IN THE UNIVERSE.
AS I LAY HERE, ON THE OTHER SIDE OF THE WORLD,
IN THE YEAR 2024, ON TOUR, AS PER NORMAL,
I PONDER MY TIME ON THIS PLANET.
I AM A WORKING MOTHER, ALWAYS HAVE BEEN.
I AM ANALYZING THE 'MEANING' OF MOTHERS DAY?
DID I DO MY BEST? WAS I A GOOD MOM?
I HAVE BEEN ABLE TO GIVE MY CHILDREN AND GRANDCHILD
A PROPER START IN LIFE,
SO, IT CANNOT BE A BAD THING, CAN IT?
A QUESTION WITH NO ANSWER.
I LIE HERE ALONE IN BED, AFTER A GREAT SHOW,
TRYING TO SLEEP BUT A LITTLE BOTHERED.
HOW LONG WILL I KEEP ON PRETENDING,
THAT EVERYTHING IS FINE. IT IS NOT.
NATURES DICTATES, UNFORTUNATELY
AND IT IS IMPOSSIBLE TO LET GO
OF THAT IMBILICAL CHORD THAT BINDS US
TO OUR CHILDREN
I WOULD LIKE TO SMACK MY HANDS TOGETHER
IN RECOGNITION OF THIS REALITY. BUT I CANNOT.
MY HANDS SMACK TOGETHER AND SAY,
YOU ARE A MOTHER, AND THAT WILL NEVER CHANGE.
HAPPY MOTHERS DAY TO ALL OF YOU WHO ARE IN PAIN.
PAIN, WHICH SEEMS TO BE AN ESSENTIAL PART OF
BEING A MOTHER.
NO MATTER WHAT A BLESSING IT IS,
IT IS NEVER PAIN FREE.

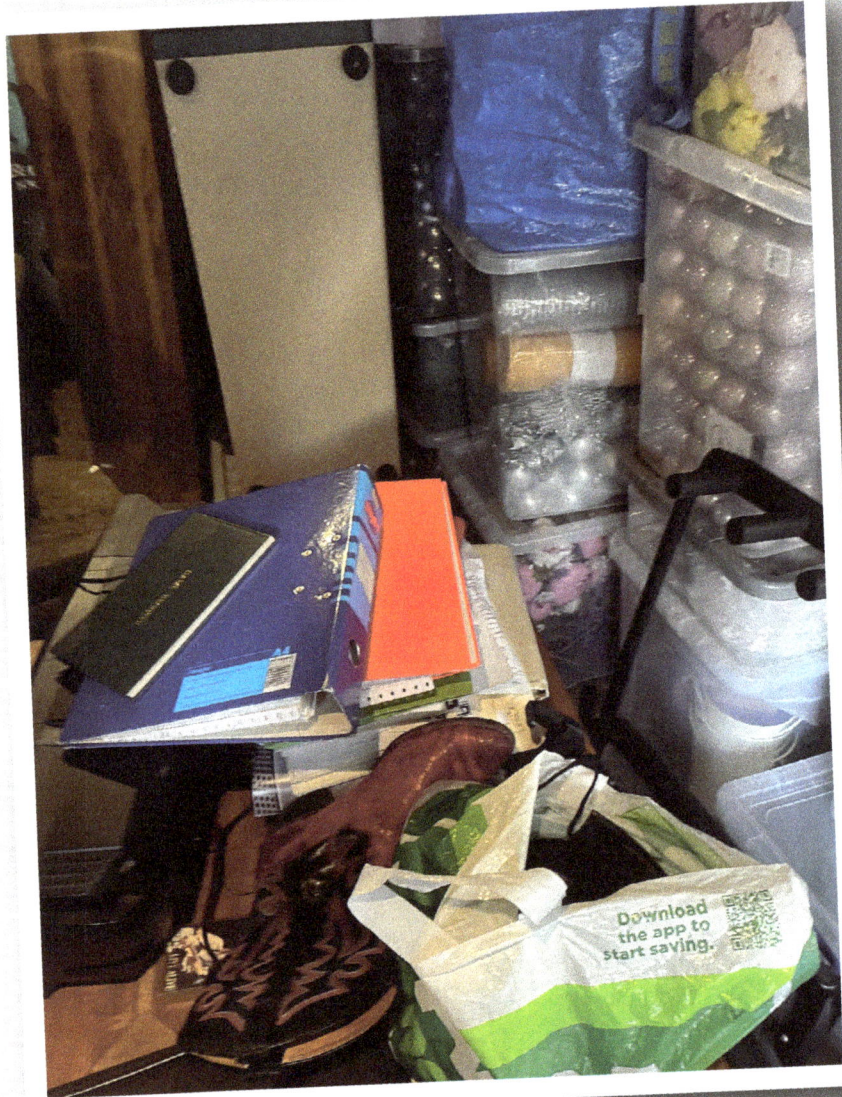

Photo Credit Austen Burrows.

After the difficult Australian tour in 2024 for personal reasons, even more difficult personal reasons were awaiting me back in the UK. I faced them all head on, and poem after poem after poem came pouring out.

I was bleeding and couldn't find a big enough plaster to staunch the flow.

THE GARAGE SALE

SOMETIMES WHEN YOU MOVE,
YOU DISCARD THE UNNECESSARY.
MENTALLY AND PHYSICALLY,
THE GARAGE SALE, A NECESSITY.

FOLDED CHAIRS AGAINST LAMPSHADES,
OVER BULBS THAT HAVE NO LIGHT
A DUSTY ANTIQUE CABINET
STANDS IN DAYLIGHT, AND THROUGH THE NIGHT.

A JAGUAR, A PAINTING SOME PHOTOGRAPHS,
A TABLE THAT LASTED THE COURSE.
PILED UP ON THE COLD CEMENT FLOOR,
THE GARAGE SALE, FULL OF REMORSE.

AS YOU GAZE OVER HIS LIFE,
IT TRIGGERS YOU DEEP INSIDE,
FAMILY, FAME, AND FORTUNE,
NO, HE NEVER HEARD YOU CRY.

THE STARK UNADORNED TRUTH,
HITS YOU WHERE YOU LIVE.
YOU DIDN'T 'LEAVE HIM, HE 'LOST' YOU,
HE HAD NO MORE LEFT TO GIVE.

SOMETIMES WHEN YOU MOVE,
YOU DISCARD THE UNNECESSARY.
MENTALLY AND PHYSICALLY,
THIS GARAGE SALE, A NECESSITY.

Our son's wedding. Beautiful from the beginning to the end of the day.

(Something written recently, not a poem, just thoughts pouring out.)

Is it true that familiarity breeds contempt?

Are there annoyances of your partner's bad habits?

In fact is there zero tolerance? The flip side is, even at your angriest, you can still see the person you fell in love with.

There is no hiding from each other, which of course is a double edged sword.

Step back, look at the scenario, count to ten, and breathe. There you go. Back on track.

THE BOAT HE ROWED

(no mystery where this came from, a poem I 'had' to write,
and it finally arrived)

SOMEONE VERY CLOSE TO ME ONCE SAID,
"I HAVE FELT FOR A LONG TIME LIKE BEING IN A BOAT IN THE
MIDDLE OF THE OCEAN,
WITH NOWHERE TO DOCK"
IT KNOCKED ME FOR SIX EMOTIONALLY.
THE SUBTEXT WAS, I WAS HIS DOCKING POINT.
I WAS HIS HAVEN; I WAS HIS ANCHOR.
I WAS HIS PLACE CALLED SAFE.
NOW ALL THESE YEARS LATER,
AND HIS BOAT HAS STILL NOT DOCKED.
TOO MANY RIP TIDES IN THE WAY.
DISAPPOINTMENTS IN PEOPLE HE BELIEVED IN AND TRUSTED.
AN UNHOLY ALLIANCE, AND CRUEL AWAKENING,
WHEN THE LIGHT WENT ON.
REALISING WHAT AN IDIOT HE'D BEEN.
FOOLISH, BLINDED, AS THE LIGHT SWITCHED OFF.
ANGRY AT THE WORLD, ANGRY AT EVERYONE BUT HIMSELF,
THE ONE PERSON WHO DESERVED HIS ANGER.
HE CHOSE THE WRONG ONES TO BE CLOSE TO, AND IN DOING SO,
LOST THE RIGHT ONES WHO TRULY LOVED HIM,
HEART AND SOUL.
HE ROWED HIS BOAT, NO DIRECTION KNOWN.
OLD AGE DOES IT'S WORST, HE NEEDS HELP.
SOMETHING HE DREADED NEEDING.
PRIDE IS IN THE BACK SEAT; NECESSITY IS DRIVING THE CAR.
ALL THOSE AROUND ARE DOING THEIR BEST TO COPE.
ITS NOT EASY, ITS NOT EASY, ITS NOT EASY, NO, IT IS NOT EASY.
IT'S A TRAGEDY WITH NO HAPPY ENDING.
JUST AN ENDING.
STRANDED WITH NOWHERE TO DOCK,
CAUGHT BETWEEN SUNRISE AND SUNSET
IN THE MIDDLE OF THE OCEAN OF HIS LIFE,
IIE REMEMBERS WHAT'S BEST TO FORGET
STRANDED WITH NOWHERE TO DOCK
DARK REGRETS, TICKING SLOWLY DOWN HIS CLOCK.

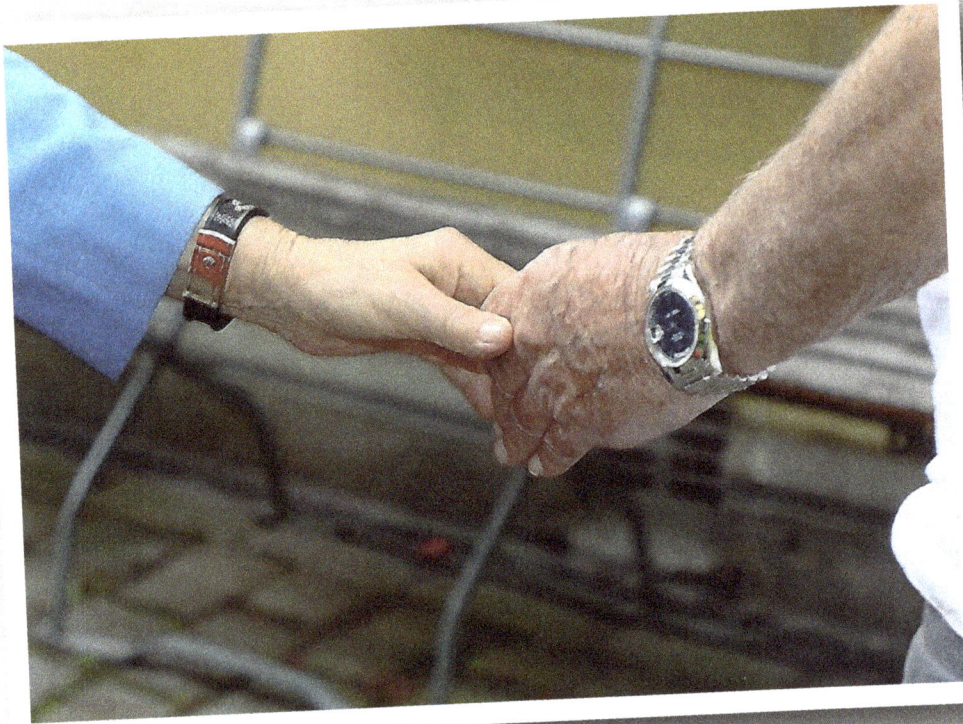

My 75th birthday party, arranged with loving care by my husband. And here we are, in our 32nd year of marriage, still holding hands. awwwwwwww

Photo Credit: Stefan Hoyer

I have been told that I am 'anal' about my own space, and I guess I am. I like my own bathroom, my own closet, my own bed, my own thoughts, my own opinions, and most important,
I like my own company.
But being the Gemini I am... I also 'need' company.
Go figure!!!

HOW SUITE IT IS

LACE CURTAINS ON THE SECOND FLOOR
A GREY DAY A GREY RIVER.
ROOM TO ROOM, OPEN DOOR, TO OPEN DOOR,
A ROOM IN BETWEEN, THE TAKER GREETS THE GIVER.
HOW SUITE IT IS.

GROWING UP IN CROWDED CHAOS,
A CERTAIN NEED WITHIN YOUR BONES,
FOR PRECIOUS THINGS THAT ARE YOURS,
YOURS, AND YOURS ALONE.
HOW SUITE IT IS.

SO SILENT IS THE SILENCE,
YOU CAN HEAR YOURSELF THINK.
FLOATING ON THIS MENTAL OCEAN,
SKATING ACROSS YOUR ICE RINK
HOW SUITE IT IS.

RELUCTANT TO SHARE THE MOMENT,
SO PEACEFUL THIS SOLITUTE,
SOMEHOW, HE FINDS A GOOD REASON,
SOMEHOW, HE WILL INTRUDE.
HOW SUITE IT IS.

ONCE THE INTRUSTION IS OVER,
LIKE A DOG MARKING A TREE,
HE WILL GO BACK TO 'HIS' SPACE,
AND ONCE AGAIN YOUR SPACE IS FREE.
HOW SUITE IT IS.

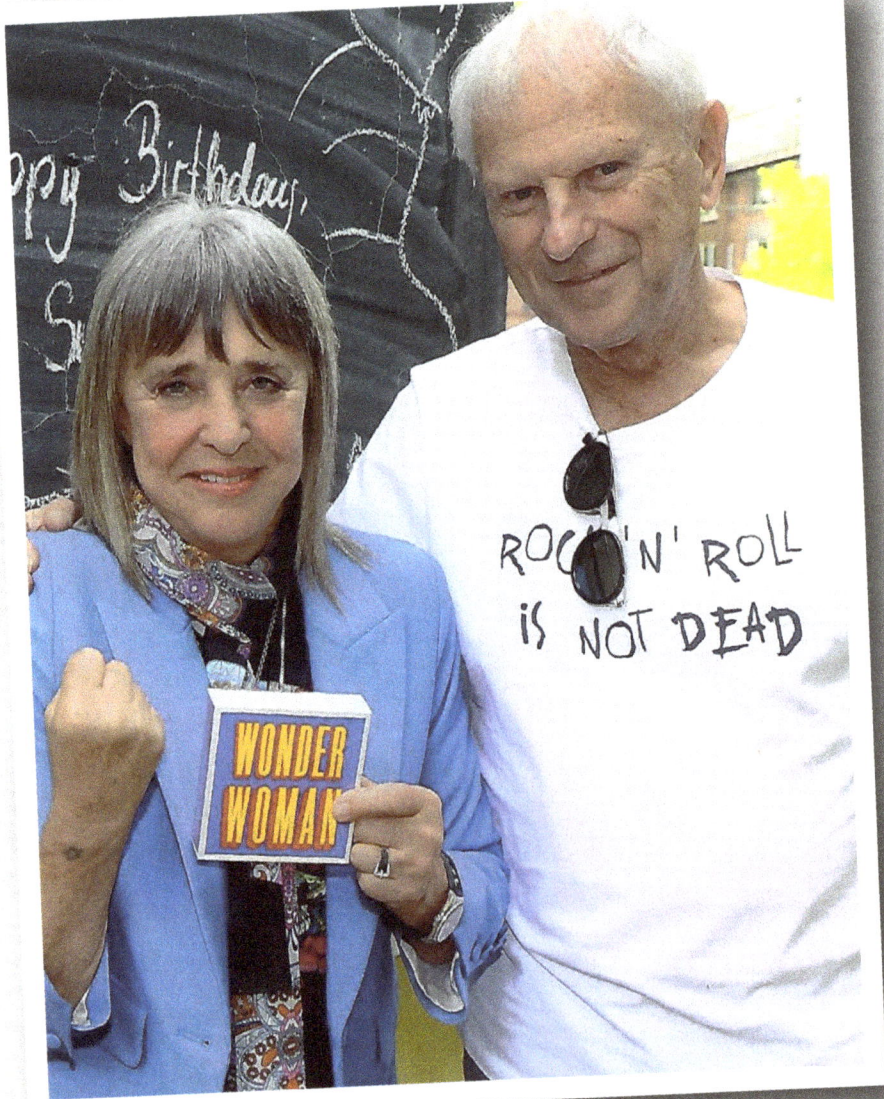

And another one from my 75th...
hilarious my husbands t-shirt and 'me' standing right next to him.

I had a house full of the Australian Team Quatro, and
I remember writing this poem, then going into the
kitchen where everyone was and reading it to them.
I did that with a few poems.

I do 'love' reading my musings to an audience, just to get
their reaction. I wonder, do 'they' remember?

THE WAY BACK HOME

IT'S NOT A PARTICULAR PLACE,
IT'S NOT A PARTICULAR PERSON,
IT'S NOT A FAMILIAR FACE
IT HAS NO LOGIC OR REASON.

SOMETHING PULLS YOU DEEP INSIDE,
TO THE PERSON YOU TRULY ARE.
THERE IS COMFORT IS WHAT YOU CANNOT HIDE
AS YOU WISH UPON YOUR STAR.

THE JOURNEY IS A DANGEROUS ONE,
MANY CRACKS IN THE GROUND ABOVE,
YOU GAZE UP TO THE HEAVENS,
AND FOLLOW THE PATH YOU 'THINK' YOU KNOW.

IT TAKES A LIFETIME TO RETURN
TO THE ESSENCE THAT IS YOUR SOUL.
IT TAKES A LIFETIME OF RESISTANCE,
TO ACCEPT WHAT MAKE YOU WHOLE.

IT'S NOT A PARTICULAR PLACE,
IT'S NOT A PARTICULAR PERSON.
YOU'RE THE FAMILIAR FACE,
YOU'RE THE RHYME WITHIN THE REASON.

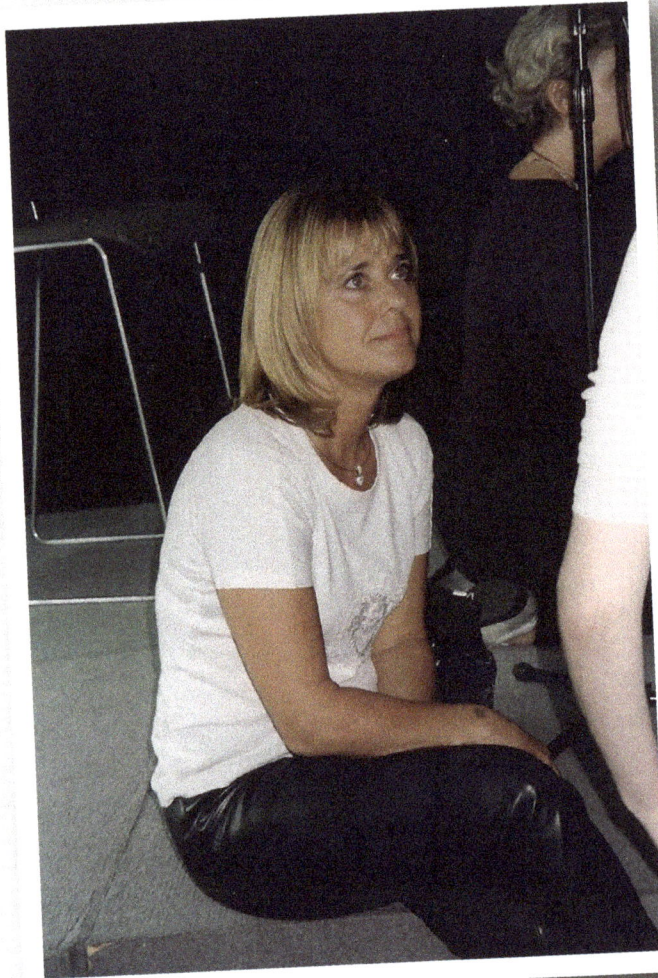

'thoughtful'. Photo Credit David Alcott

"Life is but a 'theme' sha boom sha boom",
(ref, 'life is but a dream')...

Same subject, Next stage... bad situation, but inspiration
is flying.. dated Oct 31, 2024.

As I have said many times, I need to express myself,
both good and bad. It's the way I am wired.
When I am upset, once the words go onto the page,
I can let go of the anger. You should try it sometimes.

CUPID'S ARROW

DON'T SHOOT THAT ARROW INTO MY HEART,
IT HURTS ME.
DON'T USE THOSE WORDS, THEY RIP ME APART,
AND WOUND ME.
YOU LOAD YOUR GUN WITH VERBAL ABUSE,
SHOOTING BLINDLY INTO THE AIR.
DON'T USE YOUR MACHO, IT'S A LAME EXCUSE
TO BREAK ME.
YOU CRITICIZE EVERY SINGLE MIS-STEP,
AND BLAME ME.
YOU DRAMATISE AND MIS-CONSTRUE,
JUST TO SHAME ME.
YOU VICTIMISE ME, FLEXING YOUR POWER,
SIX FEET UP, IN YOUR SHADOW I COWER,
BUT NO MATTER HOW MENACING YOU SEEM,
YOU'LL NEVER TAME ME.
YOUR POISON SEEPS INTO MY VEINS
IT'S FLOWING.
HATRED PULSATES THROUGH YOUR EYES,
ITS GLOWING.
YOUR EVIL WAYS SLIDE IN LIKE A SNAKE,
SQUEEZING MY HEART, YOU TAKE AND YOU TAKE,
YET SOMEHOW MY STRENGTH TO SURVIVE
IS GROWING.
NOW I'M POINTING CUPID'S ARROW BACK TO 'YOUR' HEART,
CAN YOU FEEL IT?
I'M SHOVING THOSE WORDS SO DEEP INSIDE,
YOU WON'T HEAR IT.
TIP TOEING AWAY, ON A WHISPER OF FEAR,
HOLDING ON TIGHT TO THAT LOVE, ONCE DEAR,
HIT ME WITH YOUR BEST SHOT BABY,
I DON'T FEAR IT.
CUPIDS ARROW STRAIGHT AND TRUE,
CUPIDS ARROW, STRAIGHT BACK AT YOU.
CUPIDS ARROW, SENT WITH LOVE
CUPIDS ARROW, IN A FISTED GLOVE.

My creation room. Nothing more to be said.

TREACHERY
(the pianist)

A BIG-HEARTED MAN CLAD IN BLACK SMOG,
ROAMING THE STREETS IN THE DEAD OF THE NIGHT.
LOOKING FOR A WAY TO ESCAPE THE FOG,
A MIRACLE, SOME HOPE, A LIGHT?

A GIFTED MAN BLESSED WITH GOLDEN HANDS,
WHO CAN SPRINKLE HIS SONG WITH YOUR TEARS.
LOOKING FOR A WAY TO UNDERSTAND,
HIS DOWNFALL, HIS SOUL, FULL OF FEARS.

MY LOST LAMB, MAMA USED TO SAY,
DON'T FORGET HIM WHEN I AM GONE.
AN NOW IT IS TO HER I PRAY,
FOR HIS DELIVERANCE, FROM A LIFE LIVED WRONG.

WE ALL HAVE A CHOICE, A PATH TO CHOOSE,
SOME MOUNTAINS, SOME RIVERS TO CROSS.
ACCOUNTABILITY COMES, WE ALL PAY OUR DUES,
OF PENANCE, NOT THE HIGHS, BUT THE LOSS.

TREACHERY COMES FROM WITHIN,
BEATING HEAVY IN ONES BREAST.
IF YOU CANNOT BE ALL YOU SHOULD BE,
YOUR BODY WILL NEVER REST.

HE STOOD ON THE LEDGE AND CONTEMPLATED,
ROLLING THE DICE, HE DOUBLED HIS BET.
THEN HE JUMPED OFF THAT BRIDGE AND PLUMETTED,
HE JUST HASN'T HIT BOTTOM YET.

Not sure where this was, in a dressing room, hanging before I start my ritual of getting ready to go on stage. Body language. Says it all.

We are connected.

There is one thing I absolutely abhor and always have done, somebody flirting with my husband in front of me or vice versa, first one or second one. The woman is trying to 'prove' she can steal my man, and if it's him doing the flirting, he's proving what??? Either way it stinks. And I won't have it. It has absolutely nothing to do with jealousy. It has everything to do with 'disrespectful'.

I would never do this to anyone. Not in my character.

NOT ON MY WATCH

FLEXING MENTAL MUSCLES
LAST ATTEMPT TO HOLD ON
BYGONE DAYS OF NO RESISTANCE
THOSE DAYS HAVE BEEN AND GONE.
SPEWING OUT, OLD AGE CHARM
SPREADING IT DEEP AND THICK
REALITY EXISTS IN TRUTH
AND THIS IS WHAT WILL STICK.
FLIRTATION OR MASTURBATION,
EITHER WAY YOU CAME TOO QUICK.
WAS IT WORTH IT TO LOSE MY LOVE
FOR A WINK, A SMILE AND A LICK?
WOO AND COO, ENJOY THE HIGH
SOON IT WILL BE GOODBYE.
ENJOY YOUR LAST HOORAH
THE COUNTDOWN OF WHO YOU WERE
RESPECT MAKES ONE STAY TOO LONG
NO CHOICE NOW, BUT TO MOVE ON.
BLESSED BE THE GOOD TIMES
THIS BATTLE WITH NO RETURN
'TIS NOTHING BUT A FOOL'S GAME
LESSONS WE ALL MUST LEARN.
FRUSTRATION, STIMULATION
INFACTUATION, REALISATION.
YES, YOUR TIME HAS BEEN AND GONE.
DUELING PISTOLS AT DAWN?
WITH AIM STRAIGHT AND TRUE
FADED EYES OF DIS-COLOURED SHADE
EXPOSING THE ESSENCE OF YOU
AND THERE'S NOTHING YOU CAN DO.
SO, BEG BORROW AND STEAL,
EMPTY MOMENTS WITH NO FEEL
DEAL, OR NO DEAL? NO DEAL.
NOT ON MY WATCH, THIS WON'T HEAL.

I'd mouth, "turn down", he would pretend to "turn down", and thought I didn't realise!! Permanantly on 11.. oh yeah.

I've said it before but I will now say it again. When I am barking, snapping, growling at your heels (5'1" now!!!), you are in no danger whatsoever. It's when I go silent then you are in big trouble. That means you have hurt me deeply and I need to recover. And when I do... lookout..

THE BIG CHILL

TONIGHT, SHE FELT IT FOR THE FIRST TIME,
CREEPING AROUND THE CORNER.
A DAGGER THRUST INSIDE
A WARNING, TIME TO MOURN HER?

SHE ALWAYS SAID SHE WOULD KNOW,
THAT MOMENT, WHEN TO SAY GOODBYE.
THOSE MEMORIES, ONCE A GLOW,
NOW EMBERS, THAT SIMPLY MUST DIE.

SHE IS FACE TO FACE WITH FINALITY
A STRANGE BUT COMFORTING TRUTH.
BLACK AND WHITE PHOTO OF REALITY
NO MORE, SWEET INNOCENT YOUTH.

THE BIG CHILL COMES TO US ALL
WE ACCEPT IT HOWEVER WE CAN.
THE BIG CHILL TOSSES THE BALL,
IT WAS OVER BEFORE IT BEGAN.

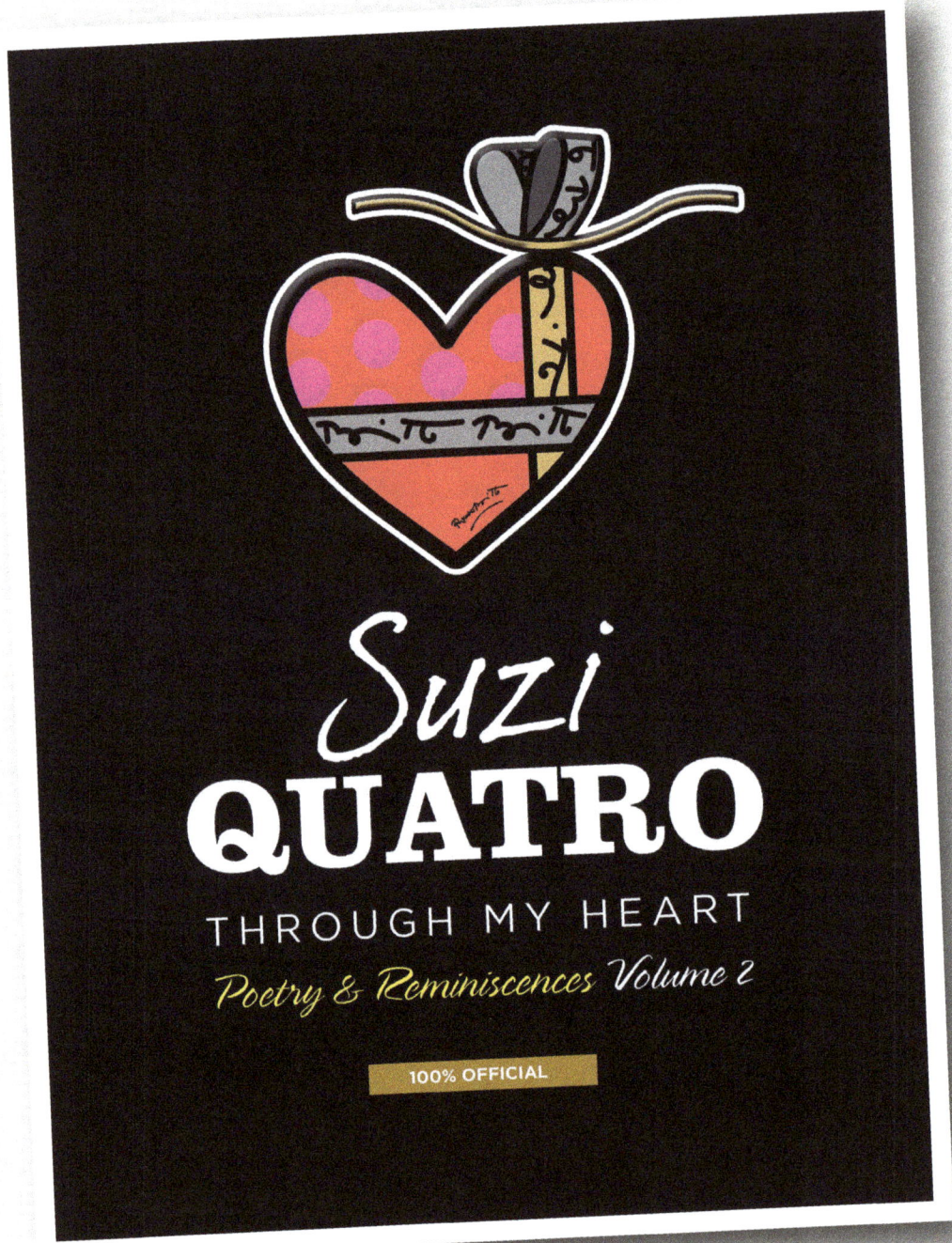

Through My Heart, my second poetry book, published in 2022.

I AM READY

SILLY A.M. WIDE AWAKE WITH HER THOUGHTS
WATCHING SENSELESS T.V.
LYING IN THE BED, SHE FOUGHT SO HARD TO KEEP,
TO SLEEP ALONE, ALONE WITH THESE THOUGHTS.
THEY BELONG TO HER, AND NOBODY ELSE.
FOR THE FIRST TIME IT FLASHED THROUGH HER MIND
SHE'S READY FOR THE NEXT CHAPTER
WHETHER A FEW LINES, OR A PARAGRAPH,
IT REALLY DOESN'T MATTER ANYMORE.
HERE IS THE TALLY GOOD AND BAD
SHE'S LIVED A DECENT MORAL LIFE.
NOT WITHOUT SLIP UPS, NOBODY HAS.
SHE NEVER PURPOSELY HURT ANYONE, THOUGH SHE KNOWS SHE HAS.
2 GOOD MARRIAGES, ONE, HER HEART, THE OTHER HER SOUL MATE.
SHE'S RAISED 2 CHILDREN, NOT WITHOUT PROBLEMS, NOT WITHOUT BLAME,
NOT WITHOUT RESENTMENT.
MAYBE SHE DESERVES SOME OF IT?
SHE IS 'NOT' A SAINT.
BUT BALANCE AT ALL TIMES.
PROVIDING A LIFE AND A LIVING,
2 GLORIOUS CHILDREN AND GLORIOUS GRANDAUGHTER,
WHAT WAS DONE WITH THESE GIFTS, NOT HER KARMA TO BEAR.
HER EXTENDED FAMILY HAVE HAD HOMES, JOBS, HAND-OUTS,
WEDDINGS, CARS,TRIPS,
EVERYTHING THEY DESIRED.
HAPPY TO HAVE NOT RECEIVED ANYTHING BECAUSE SHE DIDN'T NEED IT.
HAPPY TO HAVE PROVIDED FOR HER NEAREST AND DEAREST,
BECAUSE SHE COULD.
SHE HAS REALISED EVERY DREAM SHE EVER HAD, NOT WITHOUT PITFALLS,
WHICH IS FINE,
MAKES YOU APPRECIATE THE 'GOOD' EVEN MORE.
CAN SHE POSSIBLY DO;
A BETTER RECORD? A BETTER ALBUM? A BETTER GIG?
A BETTER POEM/ NOVEL?
A BETTER RADIO, THEATRE OR T.V. SHOW???
SHE HAS DONE EVERYTHNG THIS BUSINESS HAS TO OFFER,
AND IS BLESSED AND GRATEFUL EVERY DAY.
JUST BEFORE SLEEP ARRIVES, SHE THINKS FOR THE FIRST TIME,
IN 'THIS' INCARNATION,
THAT IF THE GOOD LORD SHOULD DECIDE TO TAKE HER, SHE IS HAPPY TO GO.
HER LEGACY IS IN PLACE.
IT'S BEEN A LIFE WELL LIVED.
SHE FALLS ASLEEP FEELING THANKFUL, GRATEFUL AND BLESSED.

"if a picture paints a thousand words"
Credit Pat Doonan

The next three were written on the RHS, 2024, in Brisbane, Australia where a lot of time was spent, a lot of solo walks taken, a lot of thinking, a lot of soul searching. I literally could not 'stop' writing. Words flowed out of me like lava, my emotional volcano was erupting.

ROOM WITH A VIEW

SIX POEMS IN FOR THE NEXT POETRY BOOK.
WOW, NOT BAD FOR A SEVENTY-THREE-YEAR-OLD ROCKER,
STILL OUT THERE STRUTTING HER STUFF,
STILL TWENTY-THREE IN HER MIND, STILL SHAKING HER ASS.
SOMEHOW HER BODY AND THE AUDIENCE ACCEPT IT.
WHICH IS A BLESSING, REAL OR NOT.
I DON'T QUESTION, I JUST SAY, 'THANK YOU'.
WANTED TO GET THESE THOUGHTS ON THE PAGE
BEFORE THEY BECOME A DISTANT MEMORY UPON AWAKENING.
IS THIS ALL THERE IS, IS THIS ALL I AM, IS THIS ALL I DO?
DOES THIS MAKE ME DILUSIONAL OR DETERMINED?
MAYBE THEY ARE THE SAME THING.
NO ONE CAN CHANGE THE WAY THEY ARE WIRED.
I AM LIVING THE LIFE, I HAVE ALWAYS DESIRED.
WHEN A NEGATIVE FORCE RAISES ITS HEAD,
JEALOUS, WITH A HEART OF STONE.
TRYING TO UNDERMINE MY LIFE'S WORK
I FEEL LIKE THE UNDERDOG WITHOUT A BONE.
DO I WALK AWAY WITH PRIDE?
OR SIMPLY GET OFF THE RIDE.
WHAT I WON'T DO IS LAY DOWN AND DIE.
THIS IS THE QUESTION I PONDER,
LONG AFTER MIDNIGHTS CHIMES,
I THINK, I ANALYZE, I WONDER,
MY WORDS, MY THOUGHTS, MY RHYMES.
AS THE RHYTHM BEATS OUT ON THE KEYBOARD
I HOPE FOR HAPPIER TIMES
NO MATTER THE MOUNTAINS I MUST CLIMB
ROOM WITH A VIEW, BRISBANE 2024
HASN'T CHANGED SINCE 1974
STILL FIGHTING THE FIGHT
TO REMAIN EXACTLY WHO I AM
THE REASON I WAS PUT ON THIS EARTH
TO PERFORM, TO SHARE, TO CARE.
TO REMAIN A PERSON OF WORTH.
THANK YOU, AUSTRALIA, GOODNIGHT.

THE BOXER AND THE BALLERINA

NO PEACE, NO LOVE, NO MORE HARMONY.
YOU SOFTLY CLOSE YOUR DOOR.
THUMB AND FOREFINGER ENCIRCLED,
CROSSLEGGED ON THE FLOOR.
NOT WORKING IS IT!
IS IT MAYBE TIME TO QUIT?

THE PROVERBIAL TOWEL
HAS BEEN THROWN ONTO THE FLOOR.
HIS GLOVES ARE OFF,
10, 9, 8, 7 , 6 , 5, 4
AS YOU JUMP TO YOUR FEET,
FORCING YOUR HEART TO BEAT.

HOW MANY ROUNDS MUST YOU GO?
HOW MANY BLOWS MUST YOU TAKE?
HOW MUCH TIME TILL YOU KNOW,
IF YOU'RE PUNCHING ABOVE YOUR WEIGHT.
BOXER, BALLERINA, OPPOSITE SIDES,
WHISTLE BLOWS, YOU BOTH HIT YOUR STRIDE.

ONTO THE STAGE, INSIDE THE RING
BITTERSWEET MUSIC IN YOUR EARS
FROM THIS MATCH THERE WILL BE NO WINNER
JUST THE SILENCE OF ABSENT CHEERS.
NO REFEREE TO PUSH YOU APART,
THERE IS NOTHING LEFT BUT TEARS.

ONE BOXER IN AN EMPTY ARENA,
DEFENDING HIS TITLE
ONE DELICATE BALLERINA,
DANCING IN DENIAL.
THE BELL DINGS, IT'S ALL OVER
FOR THE BOXER AND HIS BALLERINA.

DEJA VU

YOU'RE SO ANGRY YOU CAN'T FIND AN OUTLET.
THERE IS NO 'OH WELL', PLACE TO PUT IT.
THERE IS NO DIFFERENT WAY TO WEAR IT.
THE TRUTH IS, YOU CAN'T STAND IT. DEJA VU

IT'S YOUR SPARK THEY TRY TO EXTINGUISH,
SURVIVAL SKILLS TO RELINQUISH,
OPTIMISM MAKE IT VANISH,
LAY YOU LOW, WEAK AND FAMISHED
SUCH HURT INSIDE YOUR ANQUISH. DEJA VU

YOU HAVE THIS TALENT TO DISARM,
HAZEL EYES, SUCH WARMTH, SUCH CHARM.
IIMPACTING, SOMETIMES CAUSING ALARM,
YET YOU HAD NO INTENT TO CAUSE ANY HARM.
THE TRUTH IS YOU CANNOT CONFORM. DEJA VU

THOSE GREEN EYED MONSTERS WHO APPEAR.
TRYING TO TAME YOUR UNTAMEABLE CHEER.
TRYING TO BLOCK OUT THE CAUSE OF 'THEIR' FEAR.
WITH A NEED TO DESTROY THAT'S UNCLEAR.
HONESTY SITS ON THE END OF YOUR SPEAR. DEJA VU

LIKE A HEART WITHOUT A HOME,
BEATEN, BATTERED AND WIND BLOWN,
THE ANSWERS YOU ARE SHOWN.
YET, YOUR PEACE OF MIND HAS FLOWN.
YES, YOU MUST WALK YOUR ROAD ALONE. DEJA VU

Had to resist the urge to dress up in my leathers and stand next to it.

I've been in this business 61 years at the time of piecing this next poetry book together. I have had many situations in my career happen. Good and bad. It's the price of fame.

These next 2 poems were inspired by the same person. Such a strange thing when you are touched by someone who is in emotional trouble. It is my natural instinct to try and help. I am a good listener. Turned out to be...... My stalker,...... lesson learned!!

THE INTRUDER

KNOCK KNOCK........ WHO'S THERE?
A BLANK FACE, AN EMPTY GLARE.
CAN I HELP YOU, WHAT DO YOU NEED?
BLACK EYES, WITH ICE TO SPARE

SHALL I OPEN MY DOOR, OFFER MY HAND?
A LOST SOUL, NOONE CAN UNDERSTAND.
I SEE CLEARLY, SHE'S SO EASY TO READ.
THOSE DEAD EYES, THAT DEADLY STARE.

KINDHEARTED I AM, DO COME IN.
SIT FOR A MOMENT, LET THE HEALING BEGIN.
MANY MISCONCEPTIONS TANGLED UP INSIDE,
BLACK/WHITE/ WHITE/ BLACK/.... YOU CAN'T WIN.

ILLUSIONS OF LOVE WON'T FILL HER VOID,
NO RECIPROCATION, PAGING DOCTOR FREUD.
SLIPPING AND SLIDING DOWN HER DANGEROUS SLOPE
ALL HER OWN DOING, A PROFESSIONAL SCHIZOID.

AND THEN THAT STEP TOO FAR TO IGNORE
BOUNDARIES CROSSED; SHE NEEDED SO MUCH MORE.
A VACANT SPACE FULL OF UNSHED TEARS.
I SAID GOODBYE, THEN I CLOSED MY DOOR.

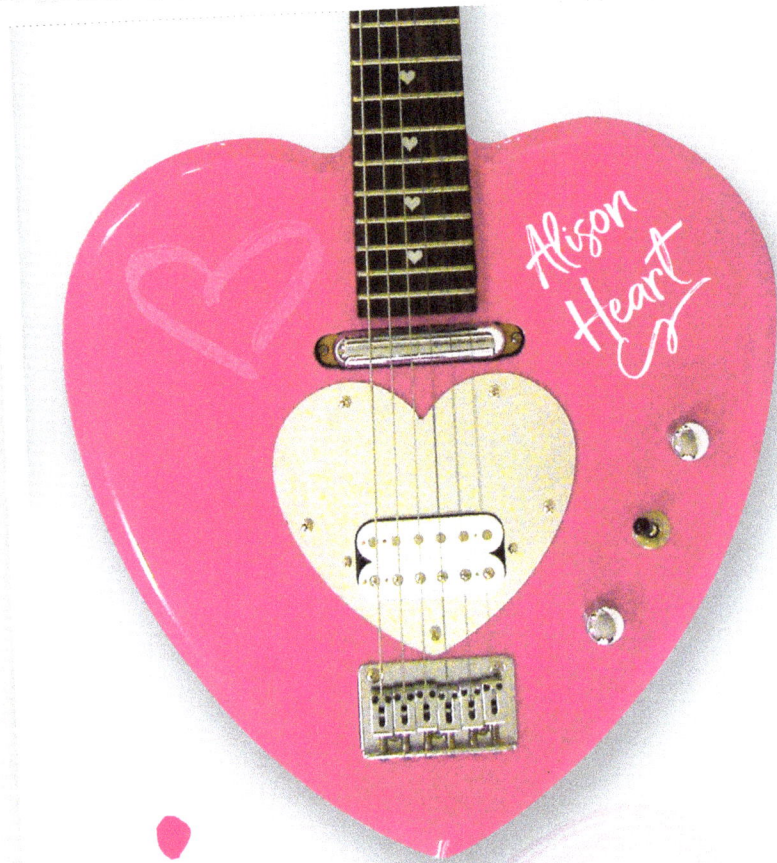

"The Hurricane", my first novel, published in 2017.

GOOD INTENTIONS

YOU KNOW YOU ARE A KINDHEARTED SOUL,
PEOPLE HAVE TOLD YOU YOUR ENTIRE LIFE.
THE WORD, NAIEVE HAS BEEN BANDIED ABOUT,
WHICH YOU ACCEPT, WITHOUT TROUBLE OR STRIFE.

YOU DON'T SEE FAÇADES AT ALL,
ALWAYS LOOKING DEEP INTO THE EYES.
MAKES NO DIFFERENCE WHO YOU'RE TALKING TO,
YOU DON'T NOTICE THEIR DISGUISE.

WHICH IS SOMETIMES A BLESSING,
AND LIFELONG FRIENDSHIPS ARE FORMED.
BUT SOMETIMES IT'S A CURSE,
WHEN THE ORGINAL VERSION GETS DEFORMED.

THEN YOUR STUCK INSIDE INSECURITY,
HOW COULD I GET IT SO WRONG?
THANK GOD THIS SCENARIO IS A MINORITY,
AND YOU CAN KEEP ON ROLLING ALONG.

SO, I WILL KEEP MY KINDHEARTED SOUL.
AND SHARE IT WHEREVER I CAN.
IT WILL TRUST MY HEART AND LET IT FLOW,
I WILL NOT FALL, BECAUSE I CAN STAND.

Doing publicity for 'Face to Face', me and KT.
We 'did' connect during the writing process, and, we 'did'
make a beautiful album together.

Oh yes we 'did'.

WHEN ALL IS SAID AND DONE

WHEN ALL IS SAID AND DONE
IT'S THE LOVE THAT COUNTS.
NOT THE FEAST, NOR THE FAMINE,
IT'S ONLY LOVE THAT COUNTS

WHEN ALL IS SAID AND DONE
IT'S THE LOVE THAT STAYS
NOT THE FIGHTS, NOR THE HEALING
IT'S THE LOVE THAT STAYS

AT THE BAR, PEN IN HAND
THOUGHTS BECOMING WORDS
TRYING TO TURN BAD TO GOOD,
IS THAT SO ABSURD?

NURSING MY DRINK, I SEE CLEARLY
LOVES' LIGHT SHOWS THE WAY.
NO MATTER WHAT PATH WE TRAVEL
I HAVE NO MORE ACE TO PLAY

ON THE BAR STOOL FEELING SAD,
I THOUGHT THESE DAYS WERE GONE.
IS IT ONLY LOVE THAT COUNTS
WHEN ALL IS SAID AND DONE?

Kids in Aussie, 1993...yep they've seen the world alright.
Credit Julie Ainsworth

NOT JUST ANY FIGHT

SO HERE WE ARE AT BREAKING POINT,
NO SAFETY PINS, OR MENDING STITCHES.
NO MORE WAY TO REPAIR THIS CLOTH,
IT'S TORN BY TOO MANY INCHES.

JUST WHEN YOU THINK YOU KNOW THE SOLUTION,
THERE ARE NO MAGIC WORDS TO HEAL THE WOUND.
AND THE 'FIX IT' FALLS FLAT, NO RESOLUTION,
ABBACADABRA, RAINS LIKE A MONSOON.

SOMETHING BROKE, NOT JUST ANY FIGHT
TOO MANY ARROWS, HIT THE MARK.
IT WAS NOT JUST ANY FIGHT
DRAWING BLOOD IN THE DARK.

TOMORROW WE MAY PICK UP THE PIECES,
BUT THE PUZZLE STILL REMAINS.
THIS JAGGED, TAINTED PICTURE,
DOESN'T FIT, IT LEAVES A STAIN.

NOT JUST ANY NIGHT
NOT JUST ANY FIGHT
NO PEACEFUL END IN SIGHT
COMMON SENSE TAKES FLIGHT

WHEN ANGRY WORDS ARE SPOKEN
IN THE HEAT OF 'WHO'S RIGHT AND WHO'S WRONG.
A CRESCENDO IS REACHED, TEMPERS BURN,
ITS AN ANGRY TUNELESS SONG.

ITS NOT JUST ANY NIGHT
ITS NOT WHOSE WRONG OR RIGHT,
THERE'S NO SOLUTION IN SIGHT
IT'S NOT JUST ANY FIGHT

The Royal Albert Hall, April 2022,
Glenn Matlock on my bass (no photo damn it),
and Boy George joining me to sing Stumblin In.

It was truly magic.

Photo Credit Neil Lupin

THE PERFECT STORM

8 YEARS OLD, COVERS PULLED UP
TIGHT UNDER YOUR CHIN
LIKE A FREIGHT TRAIN, THIS WHISTLING WIND
AND IT SCARES THE SHIT OUT OF YOU.
YOU KNEW MOM AND DAD WERE DOWNSTAIRS,
YOU KNEW NOTHING REALLY BAD COULD HAPPEN.
THEY WOULD TAKE CARE OF YOU FOR SURE,
YET THE RAIN PELTED THE WINDOW WITH DEMONS,
AND IT SCARES THE SHIT OUT OF YOU.

FINALLY, YOU FALL INTO A RESTLESS SLEEP,
NIGHTMARES OF MONSTERS DRAGGING YOU
INTO AN ABYSS FROM WHICH THERE IS NO ESCAPE
LIGHTNING AND THUNDER ROLLING ACROSS THE SKY
AND IT SCARES THE SHIT OUT OF YOU.
YOU WAKE UP TO A SUN SHINING,
SPARROW AND THRUSHES SINGING THEIR SONG,
THE ROOM IS LIGHT, WARM, WELCOMING,
EVIL DREAMS ARE NOW GONE
YOU ARE NOT SCARED ANYMORE.

FLASH FORWARD, YOU'RE AN ADULT,
WITH CHILDREN AND GRANDCHILDREN OF YOUR OWN
YOU LAY IN BED, THE SAME WIND WHISTLES OUTSIDE
THUNDER AND LIGHTNING FLASHING IN THE SKIES
AND IT SCARES THE SHIT OUT OF YOU.
THAT CHILD IS STILL WITHIN
WONDERING WHAT LIES AHEAD.
WILL SHE SURVIVE THE NIGHT?
OR WILL SHE DIE IN HER BED.
AND IT SCARES THE SHIT OUT OF YOU.

LIFE IS WHAT IT IS, COLD OR WARM
LIFE IS WHAT IT IS, A PERFECT STORM
UNKNOWABLE HURDLES, UNPASSABLE ROADS
YOU DON'T HAVE A COMPASS, YOUR MAP IS OLD
AND IT STILL SCARES THE SHIT OUT OF YOU.

This is what 'shine a light' (Face to Face, duet album
with KT Tunstall 2023) looks like in 2024 solo.

Photo Credit 'Falcon'

IS THAT A QUESTION?

(Started as 4 line facebook stanza, and ended up like this.)

WHEN YOU TRUST WITHOUT QUESTION,
IN THE FACE OF A LONE OFFENDER.
CAN YOU HOLD ON TO GOOD INTENTION,
OR DO YOU FALL AND LOOSE YOUR TENDER.
WHEN STORM CLOUDS GATHER OVERHEAD
DO YOU STAND TALL, WAITING FOR THE JOLT.
OR DO YOU CRAWL BENEATH THE BED,
AND HIDE FROM THE THUNDERBOLT.
WHEN YOU'RE AFRAID TO FALL IN LOVE
SCARED TO GO THAT EXTRA MILE.
INTO UNKNOWN ENEMY TERRITORY,
DO YOU ESCAPE OR STAY AWHILE.
WHEN YOU FEAR YOUR LIFE IS PLANNED OUT,
COMPLETE WITH MUSIC AND DANCES.
IS THE OUTCOME PREORDAINED,
NO MATTER THE CIRCUMSTANCES?
WHEN YOUR GUILT IS A HEAVY LOAD,
YET PRIDE IS THE LIE YOU DARE
DENIAL AND EXCUSES CAN'T BURY,
THE WEIGHT OF THE WRONG YOU BEAR.
WHEN YOU'VE GIVE YOUR VALUABLE COMMODITY,
A LOVING HUMANE GIFT.
DO YOU KEEP ON GIVING BLINDLY,
EVEN WHILE YOUR INSTINCTS DRIFT.
WHEN THE DARK NIGHT OF THE SOUL APPEARS,
AND YOUR MIND CREEPS TO HIDDEN CORNERS.
KNOW THYSELF DISAPPEARS,
YOU BECOME YOUR ONLY MOURNER.
WHEN, IS THAT A QUESTION,
IN ONLY'S, WHATEVER'S, WHO KNEW.
DO YOU SINK INTO FALSE DEPRESSSION,
OR FIND A WAY TO BREAK THROUGH.
WHEN.... IS THAT A QUESTION?

Soundcheck Palais, 2024. Credit: Harley Medcalf

Really loved doing the experimental dalliances on my facebook page, here is another, the result of the communication experience. It's a win-win situation. I write a stanza, post it, and then it becomes a poem. This one was the first four lines which became two.

THE BRIDGE TO NOWHERE

WHEN THE ROAD IS SO LONG, YOU CAN'T SEE THE END.
DO YOUR BURN YOUR BRIDGES OR GO BACK AGAIN?
COURAGE IS CALLED FOR, WHEN UN-ADORNED,
LEAVE YOUR COWARD BEHIND, SO YOU CAN BE RE-BORN

MISTAKES AND REGRETS ARE COMMONPLACE.
TO LIVE AND TO LEARN, IS NO DISGRACE.
LOOK BACK AT THE PAST, THEN, LEAVE IT BEHIND.
DARE TO IMAGINE, A FUTURE THAT'S KIND.

THIS BRIDGE TO NOWHERE,
YOU MUST CROSS TO SURVIVE.
THIS BRIDGE GOES NOWHERE,
BUT YOU'LL KNOW WHEN YOU ARRIVE.

HOLEY MOLEY

(more casino walks, addictive)

A NEED TO WALK THE CARPETED FLOOR,
PAST THE ORANGE COUCHES,
SO STRATIGICALLY PLACED, YET
SO UGLY.
PAST THE CASH MACHINES,
PEOPLE FRANTICALLY PUSHING MONEY CARDS IN,
HOPING FOR A WIN ON THE FLOOR BELOW,
NOT ACKNOWLEDGING THE HOPELESSNESS OF IT ALL,
'OH WELL', IT'S A NEVER ENDING 'WELL' OF POVERTY.
PAST THE UNIFORMED GUARD STANDING BY THE ESCALATOR.
NO MINORS, NO SMOKING.
STROLLING PAST VARIOUS GAMES,
ROULETTE WHEEL SPINNING, ROUND AND ROUND SHE GOES
I PAUSE AT A BUSY TABLE AND WATCH.
AMAZING HOW MANY TIMES NUMBER 8 COMES UP,
MY LUCKY NUMBER.......I NEVER BET!
THEN HAVING MY FILL OF EXCITEMENT, EXPECTATION,
DISAPPOINTMENT, DESPERATION,......LONELY,
I SLOWLY MAKE MY WAY BACK TO MY ROOM,
HAPPY I DID NOT SUCCUMB,
HAPPY THAT I MANAGED TO ACHIEVE SOME LIGHT
ENTERTAINMENT
OUT OF THE SITUATION.......VERY LIGHT.
TURNING RIGHT, TURNING LEFT, PAST THE SHOPS,
PAST THE BAR WITH A KARAOKE PIANO PLAYER/SINGER,
MURDERING 'BOHEMNIAN RHAPSODY..... OMG,
DO WE NEED TO HEAR SUCH BAD SINGING OF SUCH A GREAT
SONG?
WHICH IS WHEN I GOT SAD.
LOADS OF PEOPLE, ARMS WAVING, DANCING, SINGING ALONG,
AS IF IT WAS GOOD!!!
ARMS WAVING DANCING, SINGING ALONG, TO ANOTHER SONG I'D
NEVER HEARD.
HOLEY MOLEY, WHO'S THE SAD ONE... EH?
THROW THE DICE ONE MORE TIME... EH!
WINNERS OR LOOSERS, CHANCES ARE.....EH.
YOU DECIDE
HOLEY MOLEY.

(two five line only poems, sometimes this happens, less is more)

CHAMPAGNE

WHO YA GONNA DRINK CHAMPANE WITH TONIGHT?
HOW YA GONNA MAKE A LEFT TURN, SEEM RIGHT?
EMBERS OF LOVE, LAY DEAD ON THE GROUND.
YOU'RE SCREAMING, NOT MAKING A SOUND.
WHO YA GONNA DRINK CHAMPAGNE WITH TONIGHT?

KARMA

ARE YOU HANGING ONTO 'ME' OR HANGING ON TO 'YOU'.
IS THAT STRANGER IN THE MIRROR, THE ONE YOU FEAR,
AN ILLUSIONAL DILLUSION, YOU JUST CAN'T SEE THROUGH,
NOW YOU'RE PAYING THE PRICE, AND THE COST IS DEAR.
BUT KARMA IS COMING TO MAKE THINGS 'CLEAR'.?

I like this picture.. kind of unfathomable

I do use certain words a lot, lonely is frequent, alone is frequent, tears, pain, sadness, the truth is, I am extremely emotional, always have been, can't change it and wouldn't change it if I could.

THE LONELY ARTISTE

IN ALL I WRITE, SAY AND DO,
EVEN WHEN LIFE LEAVES NO SPACE,
TO THINK, TO FEEL,
COLOUR ME BLUE.

PAIN, MY ETERNAL ARCHITECT,
WITH ITS BRICKS, STEEL AND MORTAR,
CEMENTING CRACKS IN MY VEINS,
DESPAIR SEALS ITS BORDERS.

IF I SHOULD/COULD LOSE THIS NEED,
SEARCHING FOR THAT POT OF GOLD,
WOULD MY RAINBOW FADE TO GREY,
AND LEAVE ME EMPTY AND COLD?

I AM A POET THROUGH AND THROUGH,
CREATION BURNS IN MY ENDLESS FIRE.
MY WORDS CAN NOT STOP GROWING,
IN THE GROUND OF MY HEART'S DESIRE.

LONELY ARTISTE ARE THE WORDS I USE,
NO MATTER HOW FULL MY CUP.
FLOODING THROUGH MY TRENCHES,
YET NOTHING CAN FILL ME UP.

I REMAIN .... THE LONELY 'ARTISTE'.

AD/VERSE

THERE'S A HOLE IN MY HEART
WHERE THE PAIN RESIDES
IT'S AN OPEN WOUND
NO SCAR TO HIDE.
ALL THOSE EXCUSES,
BORN THROUGH FEAR
YEARS OF ABUSES,
ONE SILENT TEAR.
SOUL TO SOUL
LIFE'S OVER IN A BLINK,
SOUL TO SOUL
LIFE'S HARDER THAN YOU THINK.
SOUL TO SOUL, JUST LET IT GO,
GIVE A NUDGE AND A WINK,
AND LET THE BLOOD FLOOD

ALONE

I OFT' USE THE WORD LONELY,
BUT THAT'S NOT THE WORD I MEAN
IT'S THAT I PREFER TO BE ALONE,
WITH COMPANY, BUT UNSEEN.

SINCE A VERY SMALL GIRL,
IN A HOUSE OF COMMOTION,
I PREFERRED THE MIDNIGHT HOURS,
TO EXPLORE MY DEEP EMOTION.

ROOM TO ROOM I WOULD WANDER,
HEARING SNORES, COUGHS, BREATHS
KNOWING ALL WERE ASLEEP,
I COULD PONDER MY DEEPEST DEPTHS.

I WAS SAFE TO EXPLORE MY DESTINY,
MY DREAMS, MY HOPES, MY DESIRE
NO ONE TO QUESTION MY SANITY
NO ONE TO EXTINGUISH MY FIRE.

A SINGLE FLAME BURNED BRIGHTLY
BUT NO ONE UNDERSTOOD,
I WALKED MY PATH LIGHTLY
EXACTLY AS I KNEW I SHOULD.

I HAVE REMAINED THIS SINGLE ENTITY,
SURROUNDED BY SO MUCH LOVE,
I AM HUMBLED BY ONE CERTAINTY
I CAN NEVER GIVE BACK ENOUGH

I OFT' USE THE WORD LONELY,
BUT THAT'S NOT THE WORD I MEAN
IT'S THAT I PREFER BEING ALONE
BECAUSE, IT'S WHAT I HAVE ALWAYS BEEN.

Your proverbial happy ending!

I'm sure each one of you has had the experience of arguing with your partner, then a light comes on in your head, and you realise, it's all bullshit.

THE THORN ON MY ROSE

I JUST REALISED THIS VERY MOMENT,
HOW LOST I WOULD BE WITHOUT YOU.
FOR ALL MY POSTURING AND BRAVADO,
YOU'RE THE ROCK THAT ROLLS ME THROUGH.

I GUESS I NEVER HAD A MAN,
SO TOUGH, YET SO VERY KIND.
SOMEONE WHO SEE'S ME AND LOVE'S ME,
DESPITE MY CRAZY DESIGN.

WHATEVER HAPPENS TO YOU AND ME,
WHICHEVER WAY IT GOES.
I WILL LOVE YOU UNCONDITIONALLY,
HERE'S TO US, THE THORN ON MY ROSE.

(two more that started life as facebook stanzas again the first four lines that grew from the seed into this)

(no 1) THE GAME

LIFE IS A GAME
NO MATTER HOW YOU PLAY IT.
BE CAREFUL WITH YOUR WORDS,
AND MEAN HOW YOU SAY IT.
COMMENTS MADE IN HASTE
VOCAL ARROWS TRAVEL FAR.
THEY HIT THEIR MARK AND WOUND,
THEY HEAL, BUT WILL LEAVE A SCAR.
WHEN THAT STORM HAS BROKEN,
YOU CANNOT RETRIEVE.
UGLINESS, ONCE SPOKEN,
HAS NO REPRIEVE
LIFE IS A GAME
NO MATTER HOW YOU PLAY IT
BE CAREFUL WITH YOUR WORDS
AND MEAN HOW YOU SAY IT.

(no 2) DARK NIGHT OF THE SOUL

SOMETIMES YOU LET SOMEONE IN
WITH THEIR FLATTERY AND FLOWERS,
KNOWING IT'S A NO-GO WIN,
BUT IT'S YOUR NEEDED HOURS.
SUDDENLY OUT OF NOWHERE,
THIS CONNIVING DEVIL APPEARS,
TWISTING YOUR WORDS, BEWARE,
THIS WILL SURELY END IN TEARS.
DARK NIGHT OF THE SOUL HAS ARRIVED,
YOU'RE DOUBTING YOUR SANITY.
HOW IN HELL WILL YOU SURVIVE,
TANGLES IN HER DUALITY.
FRAGMENTED RAMBLINGS
DELUSIONAL DISCONTENT.
NEEDY, CRAZY, CLINGING,
IT WAS ALL SO WELL MEANT.
DARK NIGHT OF THE SOUL, OH POWERS THAT BE,
NEVER LEAVE ME IN THIS HELL.
I'VE CLARIFIED MY NECESSITY,
AND KNOCKED HER OUT BEFORE THE BELL.

'Giving 'shine a light' a whole new meaning, bulbs repaired full wattage. beautiful. Photo Credit: A. Burrows

Every artist, especially those as long in the tooth as me, goes through these feelings.

You can never take anything for granted. Every audience is a new audience and you must respect. this, and I do. They can be stamping their feet, screaming from the rafters, going absolutely nuts, and just before I walk onto that stage without fail for the last 61 years I think to myself, "God, I hope they like me tonight".

PALLADIUM/2024

ONE YEAR ON, COULD I DO IT AGAIN, AND MAKE IT ANY BETTER?
COUNTING THE SLEEPS, REHEARSING THE SHOW,
HOPING THE GOOD WOULD BE GREATER.
D- DAY ARRIVED, I CLIMBED IN THE VAN,
NERVES BEGINNING TO SHOW.
MANY TIMES, I'VE TRAVELLED THIS ROAD,
ALWAYS A LONG WAY TO GO.
IN THE DRESSING ROOM, SET UP JUST SO,
MAKE UP, OUTFITS, SHOES. DOING MY VOCAL WARM UP,
NO OPTIONS LEFT TO CHOOSE.
THE CRASH, BOOM, BANG, OF THE DRUMS,
BASS, NEXT OUT OF THE CAGE, AND I GRAB A BOTTLE OF WATER
FOLLOW THE SIGNS TO THE STAGE.
LIGHTS FLASHING ON AND OFF, TESTING ACCURACY.
MUSICIANS AND CREW, BACK AND FORTH,
IN PREPARATION FOR ROCK'S SYMPHONY.
AND FINALLY, READY TO ROLL
TEST A SONG OR TWO, FINAL ADJUSTMENTS,
TO THIS SHOW WE WILL DO FOR 'YOU'.
I PACE THE STEPS, MIC TO THE RIGHT, PACE THE STEPS TO THE LEFT.
ESPYING EVERY CORNER OF THE VENUE,
MEMORISING HEIGHT AND DEPTH.
TIME TO RELAX, AN HOUR OR TWO, RELAX! HARDY HAR, THAT'S A JOKE.
STRIDING THROUGH THE STAGE DOOR,
TILL THE FINAL SONG GOES UP IN SMOKE.
DOWN THOSE FEW STAIRS, LEAVING THE WARMTH,
NOT QUITE KNOWING WHERE YOU ARE.
A HELPING HAND, A FLASHLIGHT,
THE DRESSING ROOM ADORNED WITH A STAR.
GLASS OF CHAMPAGNE, UNZIP THE SUIT,
PEEL IT SLOWLY OVER YOUR SHOULDER
SLOWLY TRY TO COME DOWN,
EACH MINUTE, A LITTLE COLDER.
PACK YOUR BAG, IDIOT CHECK,
LOOK AROUND, YOUR TEMPORARY HOME.
ROLLING YOUR BAG THROUGH THE CORRIDOR,
GOODNIGHT, THIS GIG HAS FLOWN
BACK IN THE VAN, TOWEL 'ROUND MY NECK,
THE EVENING PLAYING IN MY BRAIN.
COULD I STEP UP TO BAT AND HIT A HOME RUN?
YES I COULD, AND I 'WILL' DO IT AGAIN.

WHEN SOMEONE...

WHEN SOMEONE QUESTIONS THE REASON YOU EXIST,
YOUR EGO TAKES A BASHING.
AN EGO YOU NEVER REALISED YOU HAD.
A VERBAL PUNCH IN THE BALLS, YEP, CAN'T RESIST.

WHEN THE OTHER SOMEONE TRIES TO DANCE CLEVER
TO AVOID SIESMIC SWINGS.
THEY REALISE THEY DON'T KNOW THE STEPS,
AND ARE DANCING TO HIS NEVER- NEVER.

THERE IS A BRICK WALL 'ROUND HIS HEART,
YET THE LOVE STILL SHINES THROUGH.
WONDERING WHICH TACT TO TRY NEXT
THE PAIN OF LOVING, RIPS YOU APART.

TRYING CONVERSATION THAT IS MEANINGFUL
TRYING FUNNY, TRYING CUTE.
INTELECTUALLY PROBING,
DOESN'T SATISFY, NOT A THIMBLEFUL.

CONNECTING ROOMS SEEM OBSOLETE
NO KEY NEED TO OPEN AND UNLOCKED DOOR.
BUT WHEN COMMUNICATION HAS SLAMMED SHUT,
NO CHOICE. BUT, ADMIT DEFEAT?

IF THERE WERE A LOCKSMITH OF REPUTE,
I WOULD CALL ON HIS EXPERTISE.
TO FIND A WAY, TO BLOW IT TO BITS,
THIS NEVER ENDING DISPUTE.

ANOTHER DAY OF DISCONTENT,
ANOTHER NIGHT COMES TO AN END,
YOU SAID, I SAID, WE BOTH SAID,
ROUND AND ROUND, TILL OUR ANGER IS SPENT.

WHEN SOMEONE QUESTIONS THE REASON YOU EXIST,
EVERY INSTINCT IN YOU REBELS.
YOU WANT TO PLEASE, BUT YOU DON'T WANT TO LOSE
WHO YOU ARE. NO CHOICE BUT TO RESIST.

THROUGH MY PAIN (pt. 2)

NEARLY 2 A.M, SATURDAY, NOVEMBER 9TH 2024,
FOR MANY REASONS SLEEP ELUDES ME.
I AM GOING THROUGH SOME SERIOUS CHANGES,
EMOTIONALLY AND PHYSICALLY. YET I AM EXACTLY THE SAME.
HOW CAN THAT BE?
THERE COMES A POINT WITH EVERYONE
WHEN YOU EXAMINE YOUR LIFE'S LANDSCAPE.
THE GOOD, THE BAD, THE UGLY,
AND EVERYTHING IN BETWEEN,
SOME BEAUTIFUL, SOME OBSCENE.
WORKING ON POETRY BOOK NUMBER 3.
WORKING TITLE, 'THROUGH MY PAIN'.
THE WEE SMALL HOURS OF THE MORNING,
WHAT THE HELL DOES IT ALL MEAN?
WONDERING IF IT'S ALL WHAT IT SEEMS.
I AM AN OPTIMIST, ALWAYS HAVE BEEN,
AND HONEST TO A FAULT.
OPTIMIST OR NOT, I HURT DEEPLY,
SOMEHOW, I STAY ALIVE,
AS I DANCE DOWN DEVIL GATE DRIVE.
TRYING TO ANALYSE THIS POEM,
THE ONE THAT WILL CLOSE THIS BOOK.
OWNING THE FEELING,
THE LAUGHS, THE TEARS, THE LOOK.
THIS PHOTO LEAVES ME REELING.
THROUGH MY PAIN, DID I WIN OR LOOSE?
I TRIED SO HARD TO BE,
EVERYTHING TO EVERYBODY,
SOMEHOW FORGETTING ABOUT ME.
NOW I NEED TO SET 'ME' FREE.
LOSE OR GAIN,
IT'S ALL THE SAME,
THE TITLE WILL REMAIN.
SANE INSIDE INSANITY
PLEASURE, THROUGH MY PAIN.
The end.. or.. the beginning.

Special thanks to who whose photos were used, and also to *Andy Jarvis* for assembling said pictures in this third poetry book. And to *Pete Cunliffe* who is not only a talented graphic designer, but truly 'gets' me.

Also, thank you to all my fans for the last 61 years who have been loyal throughout, And basically kept me 'alive and kicking'…. All my family far and wide, and all my friends.

This completes the poetry triology, *Through My Eyes*, *Through My Heart*, and now *Through My Pain*. What's on the other side, god only knows. The only thing I know for sure is there will be more poetry. That's a promise.

Suzi Quatro

Credit: Image cleaned by Pete Cunliffe

I thought this might make a cover for this 3rd poetry book , but no, it belongs here on this page. Painted in my tiny hotel room in Cromwell Road in 1972 while waiting for success to arrive. You can see the loneliness and determination in my eyes.

So confused about who I was and where I was heading.

I leave you with my love.

THE FINALE

I have done what I had to do.
I have felt what I had to feel.
I have taken responsibility for my perception
of the situation.
I have allowed myself to shed a tear
for the hurt caused.
I have admitted to myself that my ego
was wounded, and addressed the reason why.

Which made me realise, I put too high of an
expectation on our 'relationship', creating an
illusion of closeness out of 'my' needs.

Lessons have been learned.

I have dried my tears.

I have brushed off my bruised ego.

I am moving on with no regrets in peace and
harmony, perfectly in tune with myself.